Witness Preparation

A Practical Guide

Bryan Finlay, Q.C.
T.A. Cromwell
Nikiforos Iatrou

CANADA LAW BOOK
A Division of The Cartwright Group Ltd.
240 Edward Street, Aurora, Ontario L4G 3S9
www.canadalawbook.ca

Library and Archives Canada Cataloguing in Publication

Finlay, Bryan, 1941-

Witness preparation : a practical guide / Bryan Finlay, T.A. Cromwell, N. Iatrou.

Includes index.
ISBN 978-0-88804-509-6

1. Witnesses–Canada. I. Cromwell, Thomas A., 1952-
II. Iatrou, N. (Nikiforos), 1975- III. Title.

KE8460.F5 2010   347.71'066   C2010-904308-1
KF8950.F5 2010

For Carol — B.F.

For Tommy — T.A.C.

For my parents — N.I.

Foreword to the First Edition

Every young lawyer who – for good or ill – decides to make a career in litigation would like to find a way to do it well. Every lawyer who has had considerable experience in the field welcomes a convenient way to hone his or her skills and to find current expertise collected in usable form.

This is why continuing legal education in practical aspects of litigation practice is so popular. It is also the reason for the formation and operation of The Advocates' Society Institute and for the growth of moot courts at the student level.

Apart from some incidental references in the published lectures given in the C.L.E. programs of the Law Society of Upper Canada, very little has been written in Canada on the important subject of witness preparation. Thus, this book fills a gap in Canadian legal literature that needed to be explored in depth.

It is no longer possible, given the economics of the modern law practice, to teach young lawyers by the best of all methods — sitting at the elbow of senior counsel at trial. In those "good old days", you could ask your leader why he did something that worked, or why the opposing counsel handled a witness as he did.

Even with innovative practical teaching in law schools and Ontario's reformed Bar Admission Course, much of the required expertise of good counsel must be self-taught. This book brings together in highly readable form an important aspect of trial work. It can, and should, be used as a primary teaching tool and as a refresher on one or more of the subjects requiring application in almost every case.

Ever since lawyers began telling each other how to conduct litigation, the central theme has been: "The secret of success is preparation. Preparation is hard work, but it has to be done."

This aphorism is still true today. This book should make the hard work a little easier. Unorganized effort costs time and money. Use of this book should save on both.

September 1991

Hon. John D. Arnup, O.C.
Justice of the Ontario Court of Appeal
1970-1985

Preface

In 1991, the first edition of *Witness Preparation Manual* was published with a second edition following in 1999. With this latest version, we changed the title to *Witness Preparation: A Practical Guide*, in order to better convey that this is truly a book of basic principles and a practical guide, not a technical manual.

Since the last incarnation of this book, much has been written about the phenomenon of the so-called "Vanishing Trial". Increasingly, the commentators surmise, trials have become too burdensome, too expensive, and too lengthy; as a result, fewer people litigate cases all the way to trial. If the phenomenon of the Vanishing Trial is true, lawyers and students understandably may be perplexed as to why a book like this is worth reading, let alone updating.

The answer is simple. If the phenomenon is real, then a book like this becomes all the more valuable. As the preface to the first edition states, this is a book of basic principles. The best way to learn the basic principles is clearly by experience. But if the Vanishing Trial means that litigators have a dearth of trials from which to experience witness preparation, then the second best alternative is through a digestible and concise summary of the principles, which this book aims to provide.

Second, assuming the phenomenon is real, it does not take away from the need to prepare one's case or one's client. Cases may not go all the way to trial as often anymore, but that does not detract from the need to build the strongest case possible in order to achieve the best result possible for the client. The tips and techniques that are canvassed in this book are aimed just as much at building a case as they are at preparing for trial.

Developments in electronic discovery, the law of child witnesses, and the law of conflicts of interest and privilege have also required that this book be updated. To this end, we are grateful to Rebecca Shepherd and Nadia Chiesa for their research support throughout the preparation of this book.

Bryan Finlay, Q.C.
T.A. Cromwell
Nikiforos Iatrou
July 2010

Preface to the First Edition

This is a book of basic principles.

We firmly believe it is the facts effectively presented through witnesses which win cases. That presentation is an art. As an artist feels compelled to examine the techniques of others to discover what if anything is of value to be learned, so we believe those engaged in trial work may be assisted by what follows.

What we describe is what we have learned from our own experience. However, the new trial lawyer will do well to remember Robert Henri's statement to the new artist: "You can learn more from yourself than you can from anyone else."[1] This is equally true for trial work. After each time in court the lawyer should ask, "What did I learn from that experience?"

We know you will have cases where you will think you cannot afford to expend the time required to do what we recommend, or where the client cannot afford to pay you for doing it. Our hope is that you will read this book carefully (but not all at once!) and try out the methods suggested. We think you will discover that in the long run, it is less expensive than you first thought and that in many respects you cannot afford *not* to prepare your case using these guidelines.

We hope that what we have to convey we have said simply and concisely. Certainly that is the objective of all advocacy. Whether or not we have succeeded will be decided by you.

September 1991

Bryan Finlay, Q.C.
T.A. Cromwell

---

[1] *The Art Spirit* (Philadelphia: J.B. Lippincott Co., 1923), p. 108.

Biographical Notes

Bryan Finlay, Q.C. is a senior trial and appellate counsel at WeirFoulds LLP. He clerked for Justice Spence of the Supreme Court of Canada. He is an elected Fellow of the American College of Trial Lawyers, an Honourary Overseas member of the Commercial Bar Association (England and Wales), and a co-editor of *Electronic Documents: Records Management, e-Discovery and Trial* (Canada Law Book).

The Honourable Justice Thomas A. Cromwell has been a judge of the Supreme Court of Canada since 2008. He had previously been appointed to the Nova Scotia Court of Appeal in 1997 after serving as Executive Legal Officer to the Chief Justice of Canada. He practised law in Ontario and was a law professor at Dalhousie Law School, where he taught evidence and civil procedure. He received his legal education at Queen's and Oxford University. He is also the editor of *Effective Written Advocacy* (Canada Law Book) and the editor of *Preparation of Factums* (Canada Law Book).

Nikiforos Iatrou is a litigation lawyer at WeirFoulds LLP, whose practice is focused on commercial litigation. In 2009, he accepted a two-year appointment as Department of Justice counsel to the Canadian Competition Bureau. He was a clerk at the Court of Appeal for Ontario in 2003-2004, following which he was a Harold G. Fox Scholar, undertaking a pupillage in the Inns of Court in London, England. His B.A. is from McGill University and his LL.B from the University of Ottawa, where he served as the editor-in-chief of the Ottawa Law Review. He is also a contributing author of *Electronic Documents: Records Management, e-Discovery and Trial* (Canada Law Book).

Table of Contents

Chapter 8 Preparing Child Witnesses

Chapter 9 Witness Preparation and Professional Responsibilty

1

INTRODUCTION

1.1   WITNESS PREPARATION IN CONTEXT

Witnesses testify to allow the court to make the findings of fact. In addition to witnesses, the court, of course, will consider other sorts and conditions of evidence. It is the relationship among the individual witnesses, the other evidence in the case, and the fact-finding process that must be borne in mind as witness preparation is carried out.

There are two key elements of this relationship — first, the standard which is used to decide whether a fact exists, and second, the manner in which triers of fact carry out their task.

Bishop Butler may have overstated it to say that "probability is the very guide of life",[1] but in civil litigation, probability is the very guide of judicial fact-finding. In civil matters, the trier of fact does not operate on certainty, but probability. A fact exists if, on all the evidence, it is more likely than not. The adversary trial is not a scientific quest for truth, but an assessment of "what is most likely to have happened sometime well before the trial, based upon the recollections of interested and disinterested persons which are presented under procedural, evidentiary, and ethical strictures".[2]

This regard for the probable must pervade all aspects of the preparation of the case's factual aspects. The trier of fact must sort through all the evidence in the light of general knowledge of life and decide what probably happened. Francis Wellman stressed this in *Day in Court*:[3]

---

[1]   Joseph Butler, The Analogy of Religion (1756), as noted in *The Oxford Dictionary of Quotations* (London: Oxford University Press, 1953).

[2]   R. Aron and J.L. Rosner, *How to Prepare Witnesses for Trial* (Colorado Springs: Shepard's McGraw-Hill, 1985), at p. 4.

[3]   Francis L. Wellman, *Day in Court or The Subtle Arts of Great Advocates*

In preparing any case for trial an advocate should picture to his own mind clearly and fully, so far as possible, the exact circumstances which surrounded the transaction that led up to the litigation.

He should reason out where the mistakes lie, the cause of the misunderstanding between the parties, how it all happened. In this way he can discover how each witness may be corroborated on the important points in his testimony.

The circumstances surrounding a case — the little things grouped together — create the probabilities and the probabilities give colour and character to the whole evidence.

I think it was Aristotle who said, "Probability has never been detected bearing false testimony."

An advocate must remember that there are few things that can be proved in court with absolute certainty. Most trials are a battle of probabilities, as it is only the probable truth that we can expect to obtain.

How triers of fact go about weighing and assessing evidence is, in general, not governed by legal rules. The Supreme Court of Canada quoted with approval a remark by Professor Sir Rupert Cross that the process of how jurors draw inferences should not be the subject of prescribed rules.[4] However, one thing is clear. The trier of fact is not to examine the evidence piecemeal in the light of the standard of proof. Instead, findings of fact must be made by assessing the evidence as a whole and applying the appropriate standard of proof to the evidence as a whole.[5]

It is in the light of what appears probable, according to the whole of the evidence, judged by common sense and experience, that the preparation of each witness must take place. This is how the witness's evidence will be assessed by the trier of fact. Demeanour, manner, appearance and clarity of expression may all be things to consider, but the single most important factor is whether the witness's testimony fits into what Lord Devlin called "the tableau" of the evidence at trial.[6] In drawing attention to this overall sweep of the evidence, Devlin adopted the words of Mr. Justice MacKenna:

(New York: Macmillan Publishing Co., 1910), at pp. 87-8. Reprinted with permission of the Macmillan Publishing Company.

[4] See *R. v. Morin* (1988), 44 C.C.C. (3d) 193 at p. 209, [1988] 2 S.C.R. 345, *per* Sopinka J.

[5] *Supra*, at pp. 210-11.

[6] Patrick Devlin, *The Judge* (New York: Oxford University Press, 1979), at pp. 62-3.

This is how I go about the business of finding facts. I start from the undisputed facts which both sides accept. I add to them such other facts as seem very likely to be true, as, for example, those recorded in contemporary documents or spoken to by independent witnesses like the policeman giving evidence in a running-down case about the marks on the road. I judge a witness to be unreliable if his evidence is, in any serious respect, inconsistent with these undisputed or indisputable facts, or of course if he contradicts himself on important points. I rely as little as possible on such deceptive matters as his demeanour. When I have done my best to separate the true from the false by these more or less objective tests, I say which story seems to me the more probable, the plaintiff's or the defendant's . . . [7]

Self-contradiction on important points and inconsistency with the non-contentious facts are the two main considerations which MacKenna selects as grounds for finding a witness unreliable. After that, it is a matter of assessing the probabilities and asking what is more likely to have happened. As the Honourable Mr. Justice Anderson stated:

A trial judge is seldom more conscious of responsibility and frailty than when required to make such findings. In most cases, they will be final and beyond the reach of appeal. A judge has no special insight, no supernatural power to ascertain truth and detect falsehood. If a mistake is made, it is more than likely that some one of the participants will recognize that and be understandably dismayed. None of these considerations, forbidding though they are, can relieve the judge of the obligations of office. The judge must proceed with care and with the application of such skill as experience has given to do what must be done in the circumstances and to express conclusions accordingly. In approaching such questions, I have always found it useful to refer to the judgment of the British Columbia Court of Appeal in *Faryna v. Chorney*, [1952] D.L.R. 354. At p. 357, O'Halloran J.A. wrote:

"The credibility of interested witnesses, particularly in cases of conflict of evidence, cannot be gauged solely by the test of whether the personal demeanour of the particular witness carried conviction of the truth. The test must reasonably subject his story to an examination of its consistency with the probabilities that surround the currently existing conditions. In short, the real test of the truth of the story of a witness in such a case must be its harmony with the preponderance of the probabilities which a practical and informed person would readily recognize as reasonable in that place and in those conditions."

---

[7] Sir Brian MacKenna, "Discretion" (1974), 9 Ir. Jur. (2d) 1 at p. 10. Reprinted with permission of the Jurist Publishing Company.

The onus of proof in a civil case is that the party having the burden must satisfy the onus on the balance of probabilities. This has been defined by Lord Denning in *Miller v. Minister of Pensions*, [1947] 2 All E.R. 372 at 374 (K.B.):

> "That degree is well settled, it must carry a reasonable degree of probability but not so high as is required in a criminal case. If the evidence is such that the tribunal can say: 'We think it more probable than not', the burden is discharged, but if the probabilities are equal it is not."

It is with these considerations in mind that I approach the unenviable task of resolving the disputed issue in this case.[8]

It is also useful to recall another passage in the *Faryna* case[9] to which Justice Anderson referred:

> If a trial Judge's finding of credibility is to depend solely on which person he thinks made the better appearance of sincerity in the witness box, we are left with a purely arbitrary finding and justice would then depend upon the best actors in the witness box. On reflection it becomes almost axiomatic that the appearance of telling the truth is but one of the elements that enter into the credibility of the evidence of a witness. Opportunities for knowledge, powers of observation, judgment and memory, ability to describe clearly what he has seen and heard, as well as other factors, combine to produce what is called credibility . . .

These comments by experienced trial judges and lawyers are also validated by empirical study. For example, Reid Hastie and Nancy Pennington have developed what they call the Story Model of explanation-based decision-making.[10] The essential feature of this model is that jurors or trial judges construct a narrative to explain the available facts. While more than one story may be constructed, one will usually emerge as the most coherent. According to Hastie and Pennington, coherence is concerned with completeness, consistency and plausibility. They conclude:

---

[8] *Re/Max Professionals Inc. v. 804679 Ontario Ltd.*, [1991] O.J. No. 471, 26 A.C.W.S. (3d) 313 (Gen. Div.).

[9] *Faryna v. Chorney*, [1952] 2 D.L.R. 354 at pp. 356-7, 4 W.W.R. (N.S.) 171 (B.C.C.A.).

[10] Reid Hastie and Nancy Pennington, "Implications of the Story Model for the Trial Judge's Behaviour" in M.T. MacCrimmon and Monique Oullette, *Filtering and Analyzing Evidence in an Age of Diversity* (Montreal: Editions Themis, 1993).

The research we have conducted on juror decisions has led us to conclude that the juror's comprehension of the evidence is "filtered" through the construction of narrative story structures. We have identified several characteristic features of jurors' decisions:

1. Factors and conditions that make evidence easy to comprehend as a story will promote verdicts in the direction favoured by the story. Thus, the side of the case (prosecution, defense) that more closely follows a "narrative" order of proof, will be an advantage in juror decisions.

2. A juror's global confidence that the story he or she has constructed from the evidence is the truth depends on several factors:

   (i) the extent to which the story "covers" or explains the evidence presented by credible witnesses;
   (ii) the completeness of the story;
   (iii) the internal consistency of the story;
   (iv) the plausibility of the story, evaluated primarily with reference to related stories or other events with which the jurors are familiar; and
   (v) the uniqueness of the story (the degree to which alternate stories are or are not being entertained by the juror).[11]

This appears to be another way of talking about the "theory of the case" and the "tableau of the evidence".

Consider in general terms how these factors affect and guide proper witness preparation. To place a witness's story in context and to assess the probabilities, counsel must know as much of the factual context of the case as possible, including all the other evidence likely to be adduced. Witness preparation conducted without this knowledge is conducted in a vacuum for the witness and the lawyer. The witness's evidence is not scrutinized properly until as much as possible is known about all the evidence and the witness's contribution to "the tableau" is analyzed. To prepare for self-contradiction and variance from uncontested facts, counsel and the witness must carefully review all of the witness's previous statements, oral and written. In addition, all relevant documentation must be considered and the uncontentious facts reviewed. It is the considered recollection of the witness which must be placed in evidence, not the unreflective first impression. Considered recollection can be obtained only with careful attention to "the tableau". The lawyer must always be listening to whether or not what he or she is being told "rings true".

Some writers have likened counsel's role in witness preparation to that

---

[11] *Ibid.* at pp. 173-4. Reprinted with permission.

of a director preparing the cast for a performance.[12] The analogy, however, has its limits. For witnesses, auditions are rare and there are no rewrites. There are no lines to be memorized and no audience to be entertained. Instead, the lawyer is assigned to present to a tribunal the considered recollection of an assortment of witnesses whose identity is largely determined by the fate of who has relevant knowledge. Their recollection must be probed and plumbed and their contribution to "the tableau" assessed. In a nutshell, this is witness preparation.

1.2   THE PURPOSES OF WITNESS PREPARATION

Witness preparation involves two main sorts of work. First, it is part and parcel of counsel's relentless search for facts, both favourable and unfavourable. The interviewing of potential witnesses is an important aspect of this search. Second, once it is decided who will be called to testify, counsel must prepare the witnesses to give evidence, and in doing so, the duty of counsel is to make the testimony as effective as possible. In order to achieve this, counsel must assist the witnesses to deal satisfactorily with what probably will be an unusual and, in some cases, a traumatic experience. Moreover, tribunals depend on witnesses being adequately prepared so that evidence is adduced in an orderly and efficient manner. The purpose of witness preparation may then be summarized as follows:

(a) to assist in the search for the facts; and
(b) to make the evidence most effective.

A few comments about each are in order.

(a)   To Assist in the Search for Facts

At first blush, learning the facts might seem a one-sided activity with the lawyer as the learner and the witness as the source. Of course, this is an important part of the process, but not the only part. Witnesses need the assistance of counsel to dredge up all the relevant factual information available.

Aspects of memory will be lost if the witness is unaware of what is relevant to the case, if the witness's own notes or other records are overlooked or if other relevant documents are not examined. It is not a matter of the witness simply searching his or her memory to say what happened. It is a matter of the witness taking all reasonable steps, *i.e.*,

---

[12] See Aron and Rosner, *supra,* footnote 2, at pp. 6-7.

working hard, to ensure that recollection is as complete and accurate as possible.

(b)   To Make the Evidence Most Effective

The testimony of a witness must be focused. The trier of fact has a difficult enough job without having to pore over reams of badly organized, marginally relevant material. The goal of "winning the case" argues in favour of witnesses being properly prepared and centred on relevant materials before the commencement of the hearing.

A tribunal is a foreign and hostile environment for the inexperienced witness. The formality of the setting and the unaccustomed procedures will cause anxiety and induce an inability to communicate effectively. Counsel has an obligation to help the witness know what to expect and to achieve some familiarity with the process and the rules which apply. There is more to this than a cursory preparation for cross-examination. Most importantly, the key witness must be made an informed participant in the trial, not a victim of it.

2

INTERVIEW WITH A PROSPECTIVE WITNESS

2.1 INTRODUCTION

This chapter deals with interviewing prospective witnesses with emphasis on the objectives and techniques employed during such interviews. The discussion assumes that at the time of the interview, a firm decision to call the individual as a witness has not yet been made and, further, that no final view of the likely content of the person's evidence is yet held by counsel. The emphasis is on the investigatory aspect of dealing with prospective witnesses rather than on final preparation of the witnesses for giving evidence.

This structure may strike the reader as artificial. The realities of practice often dictate only one interview with a witness and that the interview must cover investigating the facts, deciding on the content of the evidence to be elicited from the witness, and preparing the witness for testimony. Even apart from the practical realities, some may find artificial the distinction between investigation of the facts and preparation for testimony. At least in the case of persons who are interviewed and testify, no clear dividing line can be drawn between the two.

There are, however, good reasons to discuss the interviewing of prospective witnesses separately from the preparation of witnesses for testimony *per se*. During the investigatory stage, counsel is attempting to learn as much as possible about the case and the witness, good and bad. The emphasis is on the completeness and accuracy of the facts and on the person's potential as a witness. On the other hand, preparation for testimony is concerned with focusing the witness on the precise matters about which the testimony, in counsel's judgment, is required, and preparing the witness effectively about those subjects. Investigation of facts and preparation for testimony are related and complementary, but by no means identical. Following is a discussion of the different techniques for furthering these distinctive activities.

2.2 GENERAL PRINCIPLES

Several general governing principles exist about interviewing prospective witnesses.

(a) Be Prepared

The fact that you are still at a relatively early stage when you are dealing with a prospective witness does not give you license to be unprepared. In order to decide whether a given individual may help or hurt your case, you must first have an understanding of what your case is about. To the extent you can, you should familiarize yourself with the file in advance of meeting a prospective witness. Doing this will provide you with the context you need in order to evaluate a prospective witness's ability to contribute to your case. Without it, you will be evaluating the witness in a vacuum.

Ideally, by the time you begin meeting with potential witnesses, you will have considered how the evidence you are seeking to gather will fit into the "tableau of evidence" we discussed in the first chapter. Other authors suggest approaching a case early on by developing "a theme" and "a theory" of the case. The "theory" is your take on how the applicable legal principles relate to the facts. It is said that a good theory of the case is one that is logical, speaks to the law, and is simple and believable. But being logically compelling is not enough. The "theme" of your case is equally important. It is how you convey the moral force behind your theory. As the authors of *Modern Trial Advocacy* state, the theory tells the judge why you must win. The theme tells the judge why you should win.[1]

Whether you conceptualize the matter of case preparation by way of the "tableau" or the "theme and theory", the purpose is the same: you must be able to contextualize the information you are gathering and determine how it fits – or doesn't fit – into the case as you intend to present it. Of course, it is not simply a case of embracing those witnesses who fit squarely within your theory of the case, and jettisoning those who do not. Rather, the interview with a prospective witness should also be seen as a way to test your case, making adjustments where necessary to accommodate newfound facts and evidence. Just as it makes little sense to interview a witness in a vacuum, it makes little sense to conduct the interview with blinders on.

(b)   Interview Everybody

The fact investigation must be as thorough as possible. It cannot be limited to key players or main observers of the important events. The context in which events took place and the motivation of those directly involved are often essential in understanding and evaluating what the key players and main observers will say. Remember, you are dealing with *probability*. A statement which on its face seems highly improbable may

---

[1]   See Steven Lubet, Sheila Block and Cynthia Tape, *Modern Trial Advocacy: Analysis & Practice*, 3rd ed. (St. Paul, Minn.: National Institute for Trial Advocacy, 2004). For an earlier discussion of the theme and the theory of the case, see D. Lake Rumsey, ed., *Master Advocates' Handbook* (St. Paul, Minn.: National Institute for Trial Advocacy, 1986), at pp. 1-4.

come to appear highly probable once context and motivation are known. Of course, the opposite is also true.

An excellent example of the importance of context and motivation assisting the evaluation of what probably happened is related by G. Arthur Martin in his superb lecture "The Examination of Witnesses":[2]

> In *R. v. Linton*, 9 C.R. 262, [1949] O.R. 100, 93 C.C.C. 97 (C.A.), the accused had killed two men, Stewart and Kipp. There had been a great deal of provocation afforded to the accused but his reaction was violent in the extreme. One of the men, Kipp, had assaulted and violently beaten Linton the night before the killing. The two men appeared at his front door at about six o'clock the next morning and said they wanted to come in the house and get some clothes belonging to Mrs. Stewart, his former housekeeper. Linton told them to go away and warned them that he had a gun and asked his immediate next door neighbour to call the police. The two men proceeded to break open the door and Stewart did get inside. Linton shot Stewart in the stomach and he staggered out on to the front lawn and collapsed. Kipp proceeded to run and Linton chased him and shot and killed him in the back yard. Another neighbour across the road was standing on his veranda and saw the whole episode. This witness testified that, after dispatching Kipp, Linton went back into the house and remained there for about five minutes or ten minutes. At the end of the five or ten minutes Stewart who had been lying wounded on the front lawn moved. Linton then came out of the house and clubbed the wounded man repeatedly over the head with a heavy rifle until he killed him. The inference from the witness testimony was that Linton had noticed after the five or ten minute interval that the wounded man was still alive and went out and deliberately killed him....If there was to be any chance of reducing the grade of offence from murder to manslaughter at the new trial it was necessary to destroy the evidence of the neighbour as to the five minute interval and to get him to agree that the whole incident took place in one continuous transaction while Linton was in a frenzy from the fear and the provocation afforded by the breaking in of his home and before there had been time for his passion to cool.

Q. Mr. Jones, the deceased Stewart was well known to you?

A. Yes.

Q. When you saw him stagger out of the house holding his stomach and collapse on the front lawn you realized that he must be seriously hurt?

A. Yes.

---

[2] Reproduced in the Law Society of Upper Canada Bar Admission Course Materials, Civil Procedure II, 1978-79.

Q. Did you phone the police?

A. No.

Q. Did you call to your wife to phone the police?

A. No.

Q. Did you phone for an ambulance or a doctor?

A. No.

Q. Did you ask your wife to phone for an ambulance or a doctor?

A. No.

Q. When you saw Linton emerge from the house with the gun and hit Stewart did you yell "Seth don't do it"?

A. No.

Q. Do you mean to say you stood there for five minutes and watched all this happening and you never raised your hand or your voice to try and prevent it or bring assistance?

A. Yes.

Q. Mr. Jones the fact is that you were not standing there for five minutes, the interval between the first shot and the striking of Stewart all. It happened so quickly that you didn't have time to do anything, isn't that right?

A. Yes that is right.

The witness's evidence in chief seemed quite credible on first hearing. However, once that evidence was carefully placed in the context of the unfolding events and viewed in the light of the witness's motivation, the evidence was, in fact, highly improbable, as the witness was obliged to concede.

(c) Interview Early

A realistic and convincing theory of the case can only be developed with a good knowledge of the facts. The earlier you acquire that knowledge, the sooner you can formulate and, more importantly, test your theory. This factor alone argues convincingly for interviewing prospective witnesses at an early stage. There is a second factor. As time passes, memory and interest fade. The earlier the interview takes place, the more likely the prospective witness is to have fresh recall of, and some interest in, speaking about the relevant events.

13

(d)   Be Courteous

Prospective witnesses are an important resource for your case and should be treated accordingly. Remember their convenience when arranging interviews. Consider going to the witness instead of having the meeting at your office. Be candid with the witness. Do not make promises of confidentiality that your obligations to your client and the law will not let you keep.

Even though you may quickly conclude that this person is not to be a witness, he or she may still have a wealth of information obtainable only through mutual goodwill. Furthermore, a person who may not appear to be a witness at the outset may later prove to be one, and a very important one.

2.3   PURPOSES OF THE INTERVIEW

There have been many suggestions about the purposes of interviews with prospective witnesses but three are significant:

(a) to discover the facts;
(b) to develop an understanding of the potential of the prospective witness; and
(c) to establish a working relationship.

(a)   To Discover the Facts

Factual investigation is probably the most important aspect of trial preparation. "Let the facts be known as they are, and the law will sprout from the seed and turn its branches toward the light."[3] Interviewing people with relevant knowledge is an important part of pre-trial fact investigation.

The first of several key aspects is that you are looking for both the favourable and the unfavourable. There is a body of opinion that in criminal cases counsel should not ask the client "what happened?", since, if the true facts are disclosed, counsel may then be ethically inhibited in presenting a particular defence. Rather, this body of opinion suggests that the client be asked "what do the police say happened?". We consider this opinion to be in error. What is essential to the presentation of the case if you hope to do the best for your client is to obtain a complete grasp of the facts, and the sooner you achieve that grasp the better. If the facts disclose little or no defence other than requiring the Crown to prove its case, so be

---

[3]   Benjamin Cardozo as quoted in L.P. Stryker, *The Art of Advocacy* (Washington D.C.: Zenger Publishing, 1954), at p. 11.

it. On the other hand, the facts may enhance an otherwise doubtful defence.

Counsel cannot preclude the latter benefit to the client by pre-empting the search for those facts at the outset.

In seeking to ascertain the unfavourable, always ask yourself: "Aside from the matters of particular interest to me, what other information might this potential witness have?" An example will help make the point. A senior architect in a major firm of commercial architects was to be called to testify about whether it was architecturally possible and economical to construct a certain building on a parcel of land. Another issue in the case, and one in which the architect was *not* to be questioned in chief, was the state of the real estate market during a certain period. Counsel's case was that the market was fair to good. After obtaining the architect's technical evidence in detail, counsel asked the architect, almost in passing, how the market had been in the relevant period. The reply was that he had been the managing partner of the firm at that time and the market was so slow that the firm had the worst results in its 60-year history. Remember, it is better to hear it first in your office than first in the courtroom.

Each interview should be used as an opportunity to check the facts as you hear them from others, as well as to elicit "new" facts. Remember "the tableau" and assess how this person's story fits with the emerging overall picture. Does it "ring true"?

Do not take a narrow view of what are "the facts". As previously mentioned, context and motivation of witnesses are crucially important.

Always look for any relevant piece of paper. Does this prospective witness have any information about the existence of relevant documentation? Remember, one piece of paper may be worth 10 witnesses.

(b)   To Develop an Understanding of the Potential of the Prospective Witness

Someone once said that we should listen to the music, not just the words. This is true of prospective witnesses. You will make decisions that affect your client's position based on your overall assessment of prospective witnesses. You must therefore not only investigate and check the facts, you must assess the potential of the prospective witness to testify creditably.

It is very difficult to determine in advance how the witness will perform at the hearing. It is hard to predict, even after extensive preparation, how a witness will respond to actually giving evidence. Some attention may be paid to things such as the witness's voice, clarity of expression, posture and demeanour. But far more significant, as emphasized above, is to assess the "believability" of the content of the witness's evidence. Here, factors such as the witness's motivation, opportunity to observe and fair-mindedness are extremely important.

The fit between the witness's evidence on the one hand, and the facts which are undisputed or appear highly probable on the other, is a crucial consideration.

Some of these factors can be assessed only after some "trial runs" with the witness, that is, going through simulated examinations-in-chief and cross-examinations. However, some important assessments may be made at an initial interview. Does the prospective witness want to please so much that he or she is overly responsive to counsel's suggestions? Does the prospective witness have respect for his or her own limitations or have a firmly held and powerfully expressed view on all matters? How truly knowledgeable is the prospective witness? Does the prospective witness seem fair-minded or intent only on "helping"? Does the prospective witness tend to exaggerate his or her own role in the relevant events? The answers to these questions illustrate the considerations that should be taken into account when assessing the witness's potential. Many of these can be considered at a very early point in your acquaintance, making due allowance for nervousness, shyness or other factors. Early impressions may be proved wrong. You should also bear in mind, however, that the trier of fact will likely meet the witness only once, and that the initial impressions will be very important.

(c)   To Establish a Working Relationship

A good co-operative working relationship with the prospective witness is important. Personal and professional respect will help induce co-operation that will make trial preparation easier and more successful. The prospective witness's goodwill must be treated as a non-renewable resource of which you are the chief steward.

The foundation of this working relationship starts with the small things such as punctuality and other basic courtesies. The prospective witness who has been summoned to attend at your office at some inconvenient time, and then kept waiting for an hour, is not likely to be in a co-operative frame of mind when the interview begins. You should be candid with the prospective witness. Do not say there will be only one brief meeting when there will be six.

You will no doubt expect the prospective witness to be thorough and give careful attention to detail. The witness will learn these qualities best from your example. If you appear unprepared, superficial or uninterested, only the most committed witness is going to persist in doing his or her best.

2.4   INTERVIEWING TECHNIQUES

There are several texts and articles offering advice to lawyers about interviewing techniques.[4] There is no intention here to offer a comprehensive or scientific approach, but instead to offer some helpful practical suggestions based on a review of the literature and personal experiences with witnesses.

(a)   Preliminary Considerations

(i)   *The Initial Approach*

How the initial approach is to be made will have to be ascertained. Whether the approach will be made by the lawyer, the client or a third party will have to be canvassed. The approach best suited to securing the interview must be adopted.

(ii)   *Legal Relationship with Prospective Witness*

A key preliminary consideration is appreciating the nature of your relationship with the prospective witness. For example, if the individual is or may become your client, the interview is or may be protected by solicitor-client privilege. This in turn may influence the scope of your discussions. In the same way, if the individual is an expert that you have consulted for the purpose of giving advice in the litigation, the discussions may be privileged. This is not the place for a discussion of the law relating to privileged communications or how the discovery rules of a particular province affect that legal position. In Chapter 5, we elaborate on certain forms of privilege, but the point is simply this. You must be clear in your own mind about whether the interview is privileged and then decide whether or not to advise the witness accordingly.

---

[4]   Some examples are H.A. Freeman and H. Weihofen, *Clinical Law Training: Interviewing and Counselling* (St. Paul, Minn.: West Publishing Co., 1972); A.S. Watson, *The Lawyer in the Interviewing and Counselling Process* (Indianapolis: Bobbs-Merrill, Contemporary Legal Education Series, 1976); David A. Binder and Susan C. Price, *Legal Interviewing and Counselling* (St. Paul, Minn.: West Publishing Co., 1977); E.L. Biskind, "How to Interview Witnesses", ch. 3 in E.L. Biskind, *How to Prepare a Case for Trial* (New York: Prentice-Hall, 1954).

(iii)   Explain your Obligations to the Witness

You will rarely be in a position to guarantee absolute confidentiality or to guarantee that the person will not be called as a witness. It is important that the prospective witness not be misled on either count.

(iv)   How Much to Tell the Prospective Witness about the Case

You will also have to give careful thought to how much you will tell the witness about the case, directly or indirectly. There is no property in a witness, and you should act as if this witness will be talking to the opposing lawyer tomorrow. Of course, you will have to adjust your approach in the light of the circumstances. You will be more candid with your client's best friend or valued employee than with someone about whom you know nothing. It is always important to consider how much of your position you are revealing and to whom, and to make a judgment based on the circumstances. You should remember that what you ask and how you ask it will reveal much about the state of your case to the person being interviewed.

(v)   Investigating the Prospective Witness

Depending on the circumstances, you may wish to "investigate" the witness before the interview. Your investigation may range from obtaining basic information about the person from your client to a much more thorough look at the witness's background. The key to a witness's potential may be his or her motivation and opportunity to observe. Any advance information you can gather will be useful in designing your approach and your evaluation of the prospective witness.

Some useful things can be done quite easily. For instance, you might do a name search through an electronic database to determine whether the prospective witness has been in the news. This may be particularly helpful if the witness has a reasonably senior position in business. An internet search for the individual may unearth key information, as may a visit to any social networking profiles or blogs that the individual maintains.[5] A

---

[5]   A recent spate of cases has illustrated the importance of conducting internet searches. Occasionally referred to as the "Facebook Factor", these cases have seen witnesses discredited by virtue of postings they made on Facebook, a popular social networking site. In particular, the personal injury defence bar has used Facebook postings to help undermine plaintiffs' personal injury claims, refuting disability assertions by producing pictures that the plaintiff posted on his or her Facebook page, showing the plaintiff engaging in physical and social activities. See, *e.g.*, *Leduc v. Roman* (2009)

check for pending actions involving the witness may be informative. Of course, how you deal with the results of these investigations calls for careful judgment, as some sources of information may be more reliable than others. But the information, or even the absence of it after a search, is potentially helpful regardless of its provenance. After all, if you are able to discover this information about the witness, it is safe to assume that diligent opposing counsel will as well.

(vi)   Environment for the Interview

A further preliminary consideration is the environment of the interview itself. Whether you meet at your office or some other place will probably be dictated by practical considerations. Particularly in the case of an important or a reluctant witness, serious thought should be given to meeting at a place most convenient to the witness. While this may be less convenient for you and perhaps more expensive for your client, meeting on the witness's home ground has several advantages. Your willingness to accommodate the witness may overcome any reluctance to get involved. Your attendance signals both the importance of the matter and your commitment to it. Finally, you may get insights into the witness when you see him or her in their home territory. A brief visit to the witness's office, for example, may give you some insights into the witness's work life, interaction with co-workers or employees, work habits and degree of success. These insights, in turn, may be very helpful as you assess the witness. As well, in circumstances where the witness is likely to have relevant documents, the on-site visit may help you to obtain and review documents that the witness may not have otherwise brought to your office.

Another aspect of the interview environment concerns the physical arrangements for the interview itself. In his book, *The Lawyer in the Interviewing and Counselling Process*,[6] Watson emphasizes that the physical surroundings must be both private and comfortable. The need for privacy is obvious, but we have observed a witness being interviewed, documents and all, in a crowded restaurant where everyone within 10 feet of the table could not help but hear everything being said. Even if the interview is in your office, some other questions of privacy remain. Should anyone other than the prospective witness and you be present? The presence of a student or associate may be helpful to you, but what is its

---

   308 D.L.R. (4th) 353, 73 C.P.C. (6th) 323, 175 A.C.W.S. (3d) 449 (Ont. S.C.J.), and the cases cited therein.
[6] Watson, *supra,* footnote 4.

effect on the witness? Do you need the presence of a student or associate to protect you from a possible allegation of tampering or for proof? What interruptions will you permit? Can your secretary come in with that urgent letter to be signed, or will you leave the room to deal with it? What calls will you take, if any? Your answers to these questions will influence the atmosphere in which the interview will take place, and these matters should be given careful consideration.[7] The goal is to inspire trust, induce relaxation, and contribute to candid communication. The physical arrangements for the interview may help or hinder achieving each of these goals.

(b)   Structure of the Interview

It is difficult to generalize about the structure of prospective witness interviews. A good deal of the literature concerns itself with how to structure a client interview, but some of the considerations that support particular structures for client interviews have little or no relevance to witness interviews. Binder and Price, for example, claim that there is no basis for suggesting that witness interviews should be broken down into particular stages, a technique that may be desirable in the case of client interviews.[8] Elliott Biskind emphasizes the need to mould the interview to the particular circumstances:

> Every witness must be treated differently; one method is not good for all. The dull and unimaginative person requires questions to be put slowly and in simple terms. The talkative and impulsive person must be held in check, yet must not be rudely or too frequently squelched for fear of offending his sensitivities. The intelligent but timid witness must be reassured. The quiet person will give you precise facts, while an opinionated one will drown your questions with his interpretation of the facts. Of course, it is the facts you are after, and unless you are rigid in your search for the facts, you take the risk of allowing yourself to accept conclusions and interpretations in lieu of hard, cold and stubborn facts.[9]

While acknowledging the need to design an interview for the particular circumstances, there are some general rules that can be advanced about the structure of a witness interview.

---

[7]   See also G. Bellow and B. Moulton, *The Lawyering Process* (Mineola, N.Y.: Foundation Press, 1978), at pp. 173-6.

[8]   Binder and Price, *supra,* footnote 4, at p. 132.

[9]   Biskind, *supra,* footnote 4, ch. 3.

(i)   The Opening

Near the outset of the interview, you should state in general terms the matter under investigation and your role in it. It is probably best to keep such statements very general. If the nature of the issue is stated too specifically, it may "bias" the witness's response and, as well, unnecessarily reveal your theory of the case. You must also explore possible conflicts of interest of the witness at an early point. Early on, you should emphasize to the prospective witness that you want him or her to tell the whole truth. You will also want to find out whether the witness has spoken to anyone else about these matters, or given any written statements.

(ii)   The Overview

Having directed the witness in a very general way to the relevant areas, it is usually wise to elicit with general and non-leading questions what the witness knows in a largely uninterrupted narrative. This approach avoids "coaching" and may help to build rapport.[10] What the witness chooses to say and not say and how it is said may also provide you with some insight into the witness's motivation, bias and powers of observation. Some specific questions may be asked, but the object is to get from the witness a narrative in his or her own words about the relevant matters.

(iii)   The Chronology

After obtaining the overview, it is often useful to go back to the beginning and take the witness through the important events chronologically. While doing so, you will press for more detail, although it may be wise not to press at this point on matters which you think are difficulties in the witness's narrative. The attempt here is to have the witness "relive" the relevant events as they occurred. It may be useful at this point to allow the witness to review any relevant documentation that may assist recollection. It is probably too soon, however, to deal with any significant conflicts between the witness's story and the documents.

A useful technique during this phase of the interview is to construct fairly specific questions based on what has been called the "hypothesis model".[11] This approach takes as a starting point that when one event occurs, a range of certain other events also generally occur. On this

---

[10]   M.J. Berger, J.B. Mitchell and R.H. Clark, *Pretrial Advocacy* (Boston: Little, Brown & Co., 1988), at pp. 69-70.
[11]   Binder and Price, *supra,* footnote 4, at pp. 125-6.

insight, one can build a hypothesis about what things are likely to have happened. This tentative hypothesis may help the lawyer to frame specific questions that will assist the witness to recall more detail of the relevant events. Naturally, care must be taken not to allow this approach to help the witness to use his or her imagination to "fill in" the blanks, but used carefully and with non-leading questions, this approach may help summon up details that would otherwise be lost.

As you work through the chronology in detail, it is wise to do two other things at the same time. First, begin to sort out what the witness knows first-hand and what he or she has learned from other sources. As Biskind said, it is the facts you are after.

With respect to each witness, it is important to begin to sort first-hand observations from surmise and repetition of information learned from others. Of course, you will want to learn everything the witness knows, whatever the source. You will also want to be more specific about the sources of knowledge at an early point. Probe as well for relevant documentation. Ask the witness about documents that he or she saw or prepared and, if relevant, the general pattern of preparation of documentation of the particular matters in issue. For example, it is useful to learn that the clerk who receives the inquiry or complaint generally completes a certain form or memo — you will want to get a copy.

Increasingly, of course, documents exist in electronic form. The rules of practice and rules of evidence in each Canadian jurisdiction, for example, provide express definitions of "document" or "record" so as to encompass electronic data and information.[12] As such, when probing for relevant documentation, ensure that computers, hard drives, databases,

---

[12]   Rule 186 of the Alberta's Rules of Court, Alta. Reg. 390/68, defines "record" as including " . . . the physical representation or record of any information, data or other thing that is or is capable of being represented or reproduced visually or by sound, or both." Rule 1.03 of Ontario's Rules of Civil Procedure, R.R.O. 1990, Reg. 194 [Ontario, *Rules*] defines "document" to include "data and information in electronic form". A more expansive definition is provided in Rule 30.01(1)(a) as follows: "'document' includes a sound recording, videotape, film, photograph, chart, graph, map, plan, survey, book of account and data and information in electronic form". Substantially similar definitions of "document" are found in: (1) Rule 30.01(1)(a) of Prince Edward Island's Rules of Civil Procedure, Reg. 492/90; (2) Rule 31.01 of New Brunswick's Rules of Court, N.B. Reg. 82-73; (3) Rule 30.01(1)(a) of Manitoba's Court of Queen's Bench Rules, Man. Reg. 553/88; and (4) Rule 218(1) of the Northwest Territories' and Nunavut's Rules of the Supreme Court, N.W.T. Reg. 010-96. See also: Rule 211 of Saskatchewan's Queen's Bench Rules, rules 284C-D and 483-4; Rule 1(8) of

and e-mail accounts are also reviewed. E-mail is a particularly useful tool in this regard. Not only do e-mail archives frequently contain relevant documents and correspondence, but by probing the sequence of messages sent and received, an individual (or the lawyer) is able to construct accurate and detailed chronologies. As "electronic discovery" becomes more and more entrenched in the litigation process in Canada, the importance of reviewing electronic records with the witness will only increase.

(iv) Working on the "Rough Spots"

There is a natural tendency for the witness to try to be consistent. This makes the way a witness relates events the first time potentially very important. As Suplee and Donaldson note,

> The first discussion of events...is likely to be critical. The deponent will likely stick to his version of the facts from the first session.[13]

If this is true, it is wise to defer the detailed discussion of crucial events until as much relevant information as possible is available for systematic review with the witness. There is no point committing the witness to a version of events that is simply unreflective recall when an examination of the relevant documents or a careful review of the basic non-controversial facts could assist the witness to a more complete and accurate recollection in the first place. The same approach is called for when you see a significant inconsistency or suspect that the witness is holding back information. Freeman and Weihofen offer sound advice on this subject:

> Instead of letting the witness get out on a limb and then forcing him ignominiously to crawl back, better use tactics that will avoid tempting him to lie. If the question is one that can be delayed, withhold it until rapport has been sufficiently established so that the witness will not feel too uncomfortable about being candid. Another tactic useful when the lawyer already has certain information that the witness may be inclined to conceal or deny is to let him know that he has it...Or the lawyer can try to get an admission of the unpleasant truth by wording the question in a way strongly suggesting the true answer. This is one of the situations in which a leading question is appropriate. Any of these devices, if they work, will save the witness from boxing himself into a position where he has to embroider his

---

British Columbia's Supreme Court Rules, B.C. Reg. 221/90; and Rule 22 of the *Federal Courts Rules*, SOR/98-106.

[13] D.R. Suplee and D.S. Donaldson, "Reconstructive Reality: Preparing the Deponent to Testify" (1988), 15 Litigation 19 at p. 21.

original perhaps impromptu untrue response with more and more untrue elaborations.[14]

These "rough spots" will have to be worked on systematically, but it is better to put off that work until you and the witness are ready. You may be able to assist the witness once you have a more fully developed sense of the undisputed facts and have made the relevant documents available to the witness.

(v) The Summary

The interview should allow time for you to summarize the witness's evidence back to the witness. This provides an opportunity to check that you have understood what the witness has said. It may also permit you to test how firm or how malleable the witness is likely to be about the evidence. For example, misstating the witness's story, or putting it in different emphasis, will allow you to test whether the witness will correct you. The witness's failure to do this suggests that either the witness is not really very sure about what was said or is amenable to "suggestions" about what happened. These are points you will want to consider very carefully as you assess the witness's potential.

The initial interview is probably not the time to confront the witness with these kinds of problems, but it is helpful to make note of these warning signals about the witness at an early date.

(c)   Method of Questioning

(i)   Not Just Questions

A witness interview must be more than a congenial interrogation. If the pattern at the interview is simply lawyer questions and witness responses, it may create an atmosphere in which the lawyer is the "boss" and the witness is the "servant". The lawyer defines what is relevant and interesting and the witness's sole job is to respond. This is not an atmosphere likely to build rapport with the witness, which in itself is a major objective. Beyond that, it may take away from the process any sense that the lawyer and the witness are co-operatively seeking the complete truth, and take from the witness any willingness to use initiative or to

---

[14]   Freeman and Weihofen, *supra,* footnote 4, at p. 48. Reprinted with permission of the West Publishing Company.

volunteer information.[15] This suggests that we should make sure the interview consists of elements other than questions, and that the questions that are asked do not relay a sense of complete lawyer control over the situation. If you compare "It would be helpful if I could learn as much as I can about X's relationship with his boss" with "Why was X fired?", the first statement relays a sense that the witness is being asked for help and that the witness is in the role of teacher, not servant. It also tends to reinforce a co-operative enterprise between lawyer and witness. The second question, on the other hand, is peremptory and limiting. It focuses the witness quite narrowly on the reasons for dismissal and imposes what may be an unfamiliar framework on the witness's knowledge. For example, the witness may know a lot about why X and the boss did not get along, but may feel uncomfortable about saying, or may not know, the reasons for the dismissal. What we mean by "Not Just Questions" is that the prospective witness must be engaged in a conversation in which he or she will hopefully become as much the initiator as the lawyer.

If you decide to call the witness to testify, you must become the teacher. You must help the witness to deal with the unfamiliar territory of the hearing and to shape his or her evidence to the relevant material, but at an initial interview, the task is mainly an investigative one. At this stage, you should do what you can to make the witness a co-player and teacher rather than an actor in a play you are directing.

(ii)   Atmosphere

The atmosphere in which the interview takes place may affect both the rapport that develops with the witness and the quality of the information obtained. The approach should foster mutual co-operation rather than a master-servant relationship.

Another important aspect of the atmosphere is the lawyer's attitude toward the witness. The literature is quite consistent in identifying a judgmental approach to interviewing as tending to block effective communication.[16] As Andrew Watson put it:

---

[15] Thomas L. Shaffer, *Legal Interviewing and Counselling in a Nutshell* (St. Paul, Minn.: West Publishing Co., 1976), at p. 119ff.

[16] See, for example, Shaffer, *ibid.*, at pp. 133-6; Andrew S. Watson, *The Lawyer in the Interviewing and Counselling Process* (Indianapolis: Bobbs-Merrill, Contemporary Legal Education Series, 1976), at p. 6ff; D.A. Binder and Susan C. Price, *Legal Interviewing and Counselling* (St. Paul, Minn.: West Publishing Co., 1977), at pp. 14-15 and 31-4; A. Sherr, *Client Interviewing for Lawyers* (London: Sweet and Maxwell, 1986), at p. 38;

... the interviewing lawyer must adopt and demonstrate a nonjudgmental, nonmoralizing posture. This means that at least consciously, he should assiduously avoid making critical comments, or statements which can be construed to be critical, about what the client has said, especially in the beginning of the relationship.

. . . . .

When counsel can bring himself to a nonjudgmental and nonmoralizing posture with the client, he may be able to listen more closely to what his client tells him. At the same time this behaviour will communicate that counsel accepts him as a person . . .[17]

It is important that the lawyer not be judgmental in attitude or response to the witness, especially at the investigatory stage. The prime objective is to obtain the most complete and accurate information possible from the witness. Adverse judgments about the witness, whether delivered explicitly or implicitly from questions, reactions, facial expressions or other conduct, may reduce the prospects for full communication with the witness.

(iii)   Form of Questions

The form of a question may affect the answer given. For example, the general rule against leading questions in chief is premised in part on the idea that leading questions might contribute to a "false gloss" being put on the evidence.[18] We tend to think that specific questions will produce more responsive, but less accurate, testimony than open-ended questions, and that leading questions will produce information that is less accurate and less complete than that obtained in response to non-leading questions.

Binder and Price, in *Legal Interviewing and Counselling*, have an extensive discussion of types of questions and their respective advantages and disadvantages.[19] They differentiate four types of questions as follows:

    (a)   open-ended questions — these are questions which allow the witness to select either the subject-matter of discussion or the

---

David A. Binder and Paul Bergman, *Fact Investigation* (St. Paul, Minn.: West Publishing Co., 1984), at p. 228.

[17] Watson, *ibid.*, at p. 7.

[18] See, for example, *Maves v. Grand Truck Pacific Ry. Co.* (1913), 14 D.L.R. 70, 5 W.W.R. 212, 6 Alta. L.R. 396, 25 W.L.R. 503, 16 C.R.C. 9 (C.A.); S.A. Schiff, *Evidence in the Litigation Process*, 3rd ed. (Toronto: Carswell, 1988), at pp. 179-80.

[19] Binder and Price, *supra,* footnote 16, at p. 38ff.

information related to the subject-matter which the witness believes to be relevant;

(b) leading questions — these are questions which set forth the relevant data for affirmation and suggest the appropriate answer;

(c) yes/no questions — these are questions which can be answered with a simple yes or no; and

(d) narrow questions — these are questions which select the general subject-matter and the aspect of the subject-matter to be discussed.

The authors believe that each form of question has advantages and disadvantages. Open-ended questions are thought to help provide a full picture, unconstrained by specific questions and to contribute to the witness's willingness to communicate.

However, open-ended questions give little guidance about what is relevant, and permit a selective and undetailed account. Such questions may not be helpful when the witness has a general reluctance to communicate. Narrow questions may help elicit more detail and may also assist in "working around" a sensitive area by using narrow questions which avoid it. Narrow questions may, however, detract from rapport by apparently taking away the witness's opportunity to explain fully or by probing too deeply too soon. Narrow questions may contribute to the lawyer "filling in". The lawyer implies that he or she knows the general picture and therefore turns to narrow questions to elicit the "details". The problem is that the general picture may be more a product of the lawyer's experience than the witness's, with the result that the information obtained is misleading or inaccurate. Leading questions may elicit accurate information where the witness knows the information but the witness is reluctant to reveal it. A leading question, asked in an accepting way, may reassure the witness, reduce embarrassment and help overcome reluctance, but because of their highly suggestive nature, leading questions may contribute to distortion.[20]

There is some research that suggests one should take this catalogue of advantages and disadvantages with a grain of salt. Marshall, Marquis and Oskamp set out to test four basic propositions, each of which is part of the "accepted wisdom".[21] The propositions were:

---

[20] This section summarizes Binder and Price, *supra,* footnote 16, at pp. 40-47.

[21] J. Marshall, K. Marquis and S. Oskamp, "Effect of Kind of Questions and Atmosphere of Interrogation on Accuracy and Completeness of Testimony" (1971), 84 Harv. L. Rev. 1620. Reprinted with permission of the Harvard Law Review.

1. The accuracy and completeness of testimony is likely to be higher in interrogations conducted in a supportive atmosphere than interrogations conducted in a challenging atmosphere.
2. As the degree of question specificity increases, the amount of material reported will increase somewhat and the accuracy of the report will decline greatly.
3. Leading questions will produce testimony which is less accurate and less complete than testimony on the same items obtained by non-leading questions.
4. Leading questions in a supportive atmosphere will produce the most errors.

The experiment conducted did not yield evidence supporting any of these propositions. The results in fact suggested that even leading questions in a challenging, as opposed to supportive, atmosphere substantially increased completeness with very slight decrease in accuracy. While this research does not address all of the assumptions about the effects of various types of questions, the results suggest that no rigid rules should be generated from these assumptions, and that there is plenty of room for common sense and experience to guide the method of questioning.

(iv)   Some Genereal Guidelines

Acknowledging that there are no hard and fast rules about the form of questions, the following guidelines may be helpful.

1. In the early stages of an investigative interview, questions should generally be open-ended. Different considerations will arise if the witness is generally uncommunicative or has a very poor sense of relevance. It seems to us that open-ended questions may contribute to the development of rapport, reduce any judgmental element emanating from the lawyer, and reduce the risk of the lawyer coaching or prompting the witness. These sorts of questions also increase the likelihood of coming across facts and information that might otherwise be overlooked.
2. During the phase of the interview when a detailed chronology is being prepared, narrow questions which direct the witness and call for details will be useful and necessary. These narrow questions should be specific, but, as much as possible, not leading.
3. Leading questions should be used very sparingly. As Binder and Price suggest, leading questions may well be appropriate where you

are quite sure of the true answer and the witness is very reluctant to volunteer the information. Additionally, the conclusion of the interview where you will seek the witness's agreement with your summary of what has been said will be in the form of a compendious leading question. Other than in those situations, leading questions should be avoided.

4. We suggest that yes/no questions have a very limited place in an investigative witness interview. Aside from clarifying specific matters of detail, the yes/no style of questioning is likely to detract from rapport and may result in a misleading picture being obtained.

(v) Sequence of Questions

There are some interesting considerations relating to the sequence in which questions are asked. As previously stated, the general pattern for the interview should be to use open-ended questions in the early stages and more narrow and specific questions as one probes for detail. This sequence is often referred to as the "funnel" or the "T-Funnel" approach.[22] Binder and Price describe it as follows:

> The T-Funnel pattern explores a topic by employing a series of open-ended questions at the beginning. These questions are used to get at the facts the client recalls. When these questions are no longer productive, the lawyer employs a series of narrow questions. The latter are used to ask about these possibilities the lawyer has thought of but which were not mentioned in response to the open-ended questions.[23]

We offer several comments about the "T-Funnel" sequence. First, the sequence is to be applied to a particular topic. It is important to stay with the same topic until you have exhausted the specific questions at the bottom of the funnel. Second, you should not move from the open-ended questions to the specific questions too quickly. The danger of the more specific questions is that they may tend to shape the content of the response.

This may introduce distortion or inappropriate emphasis on certain aspects to the neglect of others. Therefore, it is best to be sure that more open questions are not likely to be productive before moving on to more

---

[22] Binder and Price, *supra,* footnote 16, at pp. 92-100, reprinted with permission of the West Publishing Company; Binder and Bergman, *supra,* footnote 16, at pp. 295-9; M.J. Berger, J.B. Mitchell and R.H. Clark, *Pretrial Advocacy* (Boston: Little, Brown & Co., 1988), at pp. 69-70.

[23] Binder and Price, *supra,* footnote 16, at p. 92.

specific questions. Third, when you decide to turn to narrow questions, try to move from less specific to more specific rather than suddenly switching from open-ended to very specific questions. This approach will give an opportunity to assess witness reluctance to discuss certain aspects and, as well, may allow you to gain an impression about how sure the witness is of certain points. For example, if a particular detail only emerges after a very narrow question on the subject, this may be a signal that the witness is not really very certain about the answer. You will want to consider these kinds of signals as you assess the witness's potential.

The "T-Funnel", although useful in many situations, is clearly not appropriate in all situations. The "T-Funnel" sequence is designed to take a witness through a particular topic in great detail. However, as we have said before, you may not wish to deal with every topic in detail at an initial interview. For example, where you sense an area in which there is difficulty or inconsistency, you may decide to work around it until you have developed better rapport, conducted further investigation or had an opportunity to have the witness review other evidence or documentation. Dealing too specifically with a difficult point too soon may break down rapport. The general point is that the witness will probably try to remain consistent with what was first said on the matter. This suggests caution in dealing too specifically and too soon with crucial or problematic material.

The "T-Funnel" sequence approaches subjects from the general to the specific. One of the purposes of doing this is to minimize distortion which may result from premature use of narrow questions. However, in some kinds of subjects, early use of specific, narrow questions may in fact minimize certain kinds of distortions that may arise from early use of open-ended, general questions. For example, you may wish to get the witness's conclusion or obtain a generalization based on a number of observations. An example might be that a person was driving "care-lessly". The danger of inviting the witness to begin with a general characterization of the driving is that it may result in the witness framing the answers to more specific questions so that they are consistent with the initial characterization. As Binder and Price expressed it:

> If, in answering the open-ended question, the witness reaches a general conclusion — e.g., the defendant was a "good mother" — the witness's subsequent responses to narrow questions — e.g., did she feed the children regularly — are likely to conform to the witness's initial characterization.

In short, once having made a general conclusion, a witness is not likely to report individual facts inconsistent with the conclusion.[24]

In these sorts of situations, the exact opposite of the "T-Funnel" sequence may be called for. Instead, the questioning should move from specific, narrow questions about each of the underlying observations to more open-ended questions eliciting general conclusions.

(d)   Signed Statements

Most commentators urge that you should take a formal statement from the witness.[25] They offer a number of reasons. If you have interviewed promptly, the witness statement will be made while recollection is still fairly fresh. The statement will be a useful record of that fresh recollection and may contribute to the accuracy of later testimony. For the purpose of later detailed witness preparation and for the purposes of refreshing memory, the statement will provide a useful and authoritative reference point for the witness's true recollection. The statement also may provide some safeguard against the witness becoming uncooperative or changing stories; its existence makes it more difficult for the witness to refuse to testify or to change stories. If it comes to this, the statement may be used for the purposes of impeachment at trial, provided that the conditions prescribed by the law of evidence are met. Even an outright refusal to provide a written statement may provide useful material for future cross-examination.

We agree that taking written witness statements has several potential advantages, but with some caveats. In the case of an important witness in a complex matter, the written statement will be very long. The time spent on its preparation and review may not be justified by the benefits. In some circumstances, you may have decided to postpone dealing with certain crucial matters or failed to challenge certain problems or inconsistencies in the witness's evidence. If this is so, the statement will be at best incomplete and at worst inaccurate. It is almost inevitable that the witness

---

[24]   Binder and Price, *supra,* footnote 16, at pp. 133-4. Reprinted with permission of the West Publishing Company.

[25]   See, for example, W.B. Williston and R.J. Rolls, *The Conduct of an Action* (Toronto: Butterworths, 1982), at pp. 2-3; H.S. Bodin, *Marshalling the Evidence* (New York: Practising Law Institute, 1966), at pp. 21-23; C. Fricke, *Planning and Trying Cases*, rev. ed. (St. Paul, Minn.: West Publishing Co., 1957), at pp. 148-9; F.L. Wellman, *Day in Court or the Subtle Arts of Great Advocates*, reprint ed. (Littleton, Colo.: Fred. B. Rothman & Co., 1986), at pp. 79-80; E.L. Biskind, *How to Prepare a Case for Trial* (New York: Prentice-Hall, 1954), at pp. 85-6.

will remember details later on that are not in the statement. If the statement were required to be produced, inconsistency between the statement and the present testimony can be exploited by the opponent. Finally, we note a concern that the witness may feel constrained by the statement in later preparation and be reluctant to make additions or corrections, even when encouraged by you to do so.

If you decide to get a written statement, commentators offer conflicting advice on the form it should take. Some favour a statement written by you, or your stenographer, and signed by the witness. Others think the witness should write out the statement and some recommend that it be sworn. The use of tape-recorders or verbatim reporters are also suggested. In our view, the approach must suit the circumstances and the particular witness. We can imagine some witnesses who would recoil at the idea of having to write out a lengthy statement themselves and suspect that only a few would perform this task satisfactorily on the first attempt. It is hard to imagine more than one or two situations in which the services of a verbatim reporter would be called for and easy to imagine witnesses who would find a tape-recorded interview disconcerting or insulting. A more practical approach is to use the summary you have given at the end of the interview as the basis for a dictated memorandum which the witness could review and verify for accuracy. It may be important to obtain the witness's signature to the statement before you leave, in which case you will have to organize your notes into a comprehensible form for correction and signature then and there. If the witness refuses to sign, then you can ask the witness to at least review your notes and make any corrections in his or her own hand. Such corrections will be helpful if you later need to use the notes for cross-examination of the witness.

3

PREPARATION FOR EXAMINATION-IN-CHIEF

3.1 INTRODUCTION

If you have followed our advice, you now have accomplished several things toward effective witness preparation. First, you have established a co-operative professional working relationship with the witness. Second, you have a comprehensive picture of what the witness knows, both good and bad, relevant to the case. Third, you have made an assessment of the person's potential as a witness, taking into account his or her personality and temperament as well as the more obvious testimonial factors. Fourth, you have thoroughly investigated the facts of the case and, to the extent necessary, the individual's background.

With all of this done, you must now decide whether to call the person as one of your witnesses. This must be a decision made calculatedly and deliberately.

3.2 KNOW WHY THIS PERSON MUST BE A WITNESS

As a general rule a witness should only be called as a last resort. The reason for this is obvious. It is through the vagaries of even the best prepared witnesses that many cases turn. Such vagaries are probably the single most compelling reason why trial work is eschewed by the vast majority of lawyers.

The first consideration is whether you have a choice about calling this witness. You should be slow to come to the conclusion that you have no choice. Satisfy yourself that there are no other practical means of proving the matters about which the witness will testify. For example, can the same need be satisfied through documentary evidence, requests to admit, read-ins from discovery transcripts or through other witnesses who must in any event be called. There may be instances in which a witness must be called, even though the evidence is not essential to prove the case. For example, it may be unwise not to call a key player if some unfavourable inference might arise from this failure to testify. However, when you do have a choice, you must evaluate the potential of the witness.

A major factor, of course, is the importance of the positive aspects of the witness's evidence balanced against any potentially damaging testimony. Once again, it is vital to consider this potential for unfavourable evidence very thoroughly; if there are any risks that must be taken in this respect, at least the risks will be taken deliberately.

In ascertaining whether a person is to be a witness, careful consideration must be given to the role the person ought to play in the overall tableau. Unless you can articulate the need for calling this witness, do not call him or her.

3.3 OBJECTIVE

Having decided to call the person as a witness, your role now shifts from investigator to teacher. What is the objective of this preparation? It is to allow the witness's testimony to be presented in the most effective way possible. To achieve this, several more specific tasks will need to be accomplished.

1. The witness's anxiety about testifying needs to be addressed and alleviated.
2. The exact areas to be covered in chief have to be identified, put in logical sequence, and thoroughly reviewed.
3. All other relevant evidence, including documents, must be assembled, organized, and reviewed with the witness. The evidence

of the particular witness needs to be put in the context of the evidence as a whole.

4. Finally, the witness must become accustomed to the stylized, *pas de deux* question and answer of examination-in-chief.

If you try to achieve each of these tasks, you will have done all you can to properly prepare the witness for the examination.

This sort of careful preparation is an essential aspect of discharging your duty to your client and to the court. An unprepared or poorly prepared witness is not only dangerous to your client's case, but also wastes time and causes confusion in the courtroom. We endorse the following remarks of Louis Nizer in this regard:

> The law permits you – it does more than permit you, it makes it your duty – to examine your witness carefully in advance to refresh his recollection as to dates and details by exhibiting documents to him which establish these matters; to acquaint him with the sequence of questions so that the truth may be established in orderly fashion and without confusion which may throw doubt upon it. It is the only way, in fact, in which you can present the truth. For the truth never walks into a court room. It never flies in through the window. It must be dragged in by you through evidence . . .[1]

Nizer's image of dragging in the truth captures the simple fact that proper preparation is hard work – work that is an advocate's duty to undertake.

Of course, not every witness can receive perfect and complete preparation. The economics of litigation and realities of time-limitations make that impossible. We suggest that you categorize witnesses as being either major or minor for the purposes of preparation.

A major witness is one whose evidence on certain issues must be believed. A minor witness is one who is called to prove a fact about which there is little or no controversy or to prove a matter in controversy which, although of importance, does not have the potential to defeat the case.

(a) The Minor Witness

The preparation of a minor witness poses no unusual problems. However, the lawyer must determine whether the witness poses a risk from any other quarter. If such a risk is ascertained then the appropriate preparation must certainly be undertaken.

---

[1] L. Nizer, "The Art of the Jury Trial" (1946), 32 Cornell L.Q. 59 at p. 66.

(b)   The Major Witness

The preparation of a major witness is a very substantial undertaking. A key witness in a large case may require months of preparation. In most cases the key witnesses will be readily apparent. However, they may very well not include the client. Consequently, the approach to and enlisting of their assistance will require tact and, above all, honesty as to what is being asked of them.

A special consideration comes into play when a major witness is not your client:

1. The appropriate remuneration for the time to be spent in preparation will have to be settled. The arrangement must be for a fee for time spent as opposed to a piece of the "equity" since the latter gives the witness an interest in the litigation which may be unlawful and will always adversely affect his or her credibility.
2. The financial arrangement must then be reduced to writing so that the agreement can be introduced as an exhibit at trial.

3.4   PREPARING YOURSELF[2]

Before you can begin effective preparation of the witness, you must be properly prepared yourself. You need a clear idea of your theory of the case, all of the facts likely to be proved or attempted to be proved, and where the particular witness fits into the larger picture. You need to know exactly what points you plan to prove through this witness's evidence, which exhibits the witness will prove or otherwise testify about, and the sequence in which the various subjects will be canvassed.

This may seem trite. It is not. It is pointless to spend time in preparation of a witness if you do not have a complete grasp of what you understand to be the issues and the facts.

Your role is much like that of a teacher, and a good teacher must have a thorough knowledge of the subject-matter. A good teacher also foresees the difficult places and is prepared to deal with them. If you anticipate objections to the admissibility of particular items of evidence, now is the time to get your law ready and to consider alternative methods of proof. If you see problems of credibility arising from contradictions or inherent improbability, now is the time to find ways of dealing with them.

All of this takes time. A major challenge is to find that time well in advance of trial. Once the case is called, or is underway, there is rarely

---

[2]   This section is concerned primarily with the preparation of a major witness.

time for the sort of work required for careful preparation. Whatever time is available at the last minute will be needed for the inevitable emergencies and final run throughs with key witnesses. An important aspect of preparing yourself is to ensure that you have sufficient time available to do what should be done.

3.5   THE WITNESS AS A PERSON

(a)   Treat Witnesses like Precious, Non-Renewable Resources

Through the investigation stage, we suggest that you take all reasonable steps to establish a good working rapport with the witness, while at the same time beginning to assess the witness's personality and motivation. As the focus moves away from investigation toward preparation for testimony, the human element becomes even more important.

Sonya Hamlin, a consultant in communications skills, emphasizes the importance of addressing the witness as a person in her article "Preparing a Witness to Testify".[3]

She notes that the witness is likely to have considerable anxiety about the process and his or her role in it. The witness may be concerned about "performing in public", about the importance of the matter and the consequences of a poor performance. Rather than dismissing these feelings, Hamlin suggests that they need to be identified and dealt with systematically. As fear of the unknown may be a major source of anxiety, careful explanation of the witness's role, visiting the courtroom, doing simulated examinations and demonstrating how counsel may be able to assist during the examination may address the most serious worries of the witness. Hamlin also suggests that counsel must be careful to be positive in his or her approach, even when being critical. It is also vital not to "spook" the witness by being overly critical or through unduly aggressive preparation.

There are also other more mundane matters to be considered. You will need to get sufficient of the witness's time in order to do thorough preparation. You should provide the witness with a realistic assessment of how much time will be needed and make sure that the witness has allowed for this in his or her schedule. Fear of the unknown will often be a

---

[3]   (1985), 71 A.B.A.J. 80.

powerful motivation for the witness to co-operate and planning preparation sessions well in advance will make it easier to find the time.

Given the length of time a case waits for trial in many jurisdictions, you will need to keep in regular contact with your witnesses. One writer suggests a diary system to ensure contact at least every six months.[4]

While that may not be necessary in all cases, it is important to keep witnesses apprised of the status of the case and to attempt to hold their co-operation until trial. There are also good organizational reasons for maintaining regular contact. You will need current addresses and telephone numbers for all your witnesses.

As a case nears trial, you should be as thoughtful of the witness's time as prudence allows. An honest attempt to inconvenience the witness as little as possible, coupled with an explanation of the practical problems of predicting when the witness will be required at trial, should go a long way toward maintaining goodwill.

(b)   Know the Witness's Weaknesses

Every witness has weaknesses. You do not want to have to learn about these weaknesses for the first time when the witness is in the box. The weakness may involve personal traits (*e.g.*, a smart alec) or relate directly to the evidence. Insofar as the weakness relates to a personal trait, the lawyer must address the problem directly. The lawyer owes a duty to both the client and the witness to be brutally frank on these questions. In many situations, the witness can be told of the problem and the need to correct it for the witness box. The correction must take place and the lawyer must see that it is done. Inability to correct the problem will give rise to other considerations. These considerations relate to how to minimize the impact. They may include changing the order of the witnesses or the particular focus of the evidence to be given. Creativity will often be required.

For example, a particular friendly witness who must be called to describe a particular meeting is also a highly qualified engineer who could give expert evidence on issues raised in the action. However, as counsel, you know that she would make a poor expert witness with the potential to do irreparable damage. Consequently, without mincing words, you must tell her exactly the area to stay within, and no matter how tempted she may

---

[4]   Dianne J. Weaver, "Direct Examination: How to Prepare for a Successful Court Appearance" in J.N. Warsaw, ed., *Women Trial Lawyers: How They Succeed in Practice and in the Courtroom* (Englewood Cliffs, N.J.: Prentice-Hall, 1987), at pp. 137-42.

be, she must not stray unless forced to do so by a specific question being put to her in cross-examination.

Weaknesses in the evidence should also be addressed, and to the extent possible, neutralized or mitigated. Insofar as there are "soft spots" that you anticipate your opponent will exploit, you should develop a strategy for addressing these soft spots in chief. In a nutshell, if you do not bring it up, you can bet your well prepared opponent will. Much better that you take charge of these bad facts, by introducing unfavourable evidence in as positive a light as possible. The alternative sitting back and waiting for opposing counsel to elicit the information in cross-examination is certainly a less predictable, and likely a more harmful, approach to dealing with these bad facts.

(c)   Know the Witness's Strengths

It will be a rare witness who does not show some redeeming quality. The particular strength must be ascertained and, if possible, used to enhance the overall story. The particular strength may be found in an aspect of the actual evidence to be given or in some personal trait. The lawyer must be always on the look-out — more accurately, the lawyer must be listening continually to every aspect of the case. Through this process, the lawyer will become aware of clues which may assist in discovering a particular strength or, for that matter, a particular weakness. Remember, most witnesses are honest and will answer questions truthfully when giving evidence under oath. However, the ability to observe, recollect, and convey one's recollection varies from witness to witness, with the result that two equally honest witnesses may have vastly divergent recollections of the same event.

(d)   How do I Want this Witness to be Perceived by the Judge?

The purpose of all that has gone before is to aid in the most persuasive presentation of the client's story. Lawyers like to think that they actually win or lose cases. They are wrong. Facts win or lose cases or, rather, facts should win or lose cases. The lawyer must do everything within the rules to marshal, focus and polish the facts so that the client's story is most compelling. The lawyer must not, on any account, get in the way of those facts in support of the client's case.

In looking at the witness list, the lawyer is much like an admiral. It is for the lawyer to determine when and how the ships are to be put into the battle. Thoughtful planning and execution are mandatory. For example, you may have a witness who is not key but who could go ahead of a key witness and draw the first major cross-examination so that you can learn what the other side's approach to the cross-examination will be before you commit a capital ship to the battle. You may have a number of expert witnesses and you may organize them so that you call the slower, less colourful, but more detailed expert to do the "crumbling" of the enemy's position and open up the hole in the enemy's line through which the more expressive and dynamic experts will move. You may decide to call the key witness first in order to nail your colours to the top of the mast from the outset, knowing, that given the facts of the case, you must seize the initiative from the outset and never lose it if you are to have any chance of success. In short, each particular witness is only part of the larger battle.

The role to be played will depend on the evidence to be given and the strengths and weaknesses of the witness.

3.6   WORKING THROUGH THE MATERIAL

(a)   Preparation for the Examination is Hard Work

Preparation of a major witness to give evidence requires hard work on the lawyer's part. The lawyer must be prepared to spend hours with the witness in reviewing documents and piecing together the facts. The witness must be enlisted to become a willing participant. A committed witness may become a great source of information and ideas and prove indispensable to the preparation of the case.

The preparation of major witnesses should not be left to junior members of the legal team. The responsibility is that of the leaders and the reason is simple. Those who know the big picture are the only ones who are in a position to properly prepare the witness. Also remember, preparation is a two-way street. Not only is the witness prepared, but so is counsel. In preparing your major witnesses, you will come to better understand your case and the evidence to be presented or confronted.

(b)   Develop in the Witness a Respect for the Facts

Just as a sailor learns by experience to respect the sea, so should a witness learn to respect the facts. But this respect must be learned prior to entering the witness box, not while occupying it. It must be learned from you. Be rigorous with the witness. Often, the initial and unreflective memory will not be accurate. Only when the witness is fully aware of all of the surrounding details and matters which can assist his or her recollection will the witness be able to ascertain what was actually said and done. Of course, it is important for you to emphasize to witnesses that their primary obligation is to tell the truth to the best of their recollection. Recollection, however, must be informed and refreshed by all available information.

(c)   Review the Transcripts and Documents

All transcripts of previous testimony and any other statements that the witness has made should be reviewed by the witness, both to refresh memory, and to ascertain whether there are any areas in which present recollection is different than that spoken about on previous occasions. Pleadings, affidavits and transcripts in other cases in which the witness has been involved, and which in any way relate to the matters in issue in the present proceedings, should be reviewed by and with the witness.

A common book of exhibits must be prepared. At the time of the witness preparation, this will exist in draft form. The witness must be given a copy of the draft insofar as it relates to the evidence to be given. The witness is then in a position to take home this copy to review at leisure. Further, the witness will become comfortable with the handling of the documents in this fashion.

(d)   Anticipate Conflicts in the Evidence

It will often be apparent to you during the preparation that the evidence of your witness will, or may, clash with earlier evidence of the witness or other evidence to be given at the trial.

The witness should be advised how to handle any question directed to an apparent contradiction between present and past testimony or statements. You should review the difference in recollection with the witness carefully to make sure that your witness is firm in his or her recollection notwithstanding the clash. Some inconsistency with other trial evidence should not cause too much concern, but any inconsistency on a major point or on any matter which seems at odds with the overall "tableau" of the evidence as you expect it to unfold should be reviewed thoroughly. The rigour of the preparation itself may explain why the present reflection is different and better. The preparation for giving evidence at the trial will usually be much more detailed given the additional documentation that has been produced and the opportunity to review the transcripts since the earlier testimony. The earlier testimony may well have been believed to be accurate when given, but now the witness's recollection is as given in the present testimony.

(e) Review the Order of the Evidence with the Witness

You should reduce the examination you propose to conduct to your notebook and make sure that the witness has a good sense of how that examination will flow from area to area. The key areas should be reviewed in depth so that the witness has a good sense of the critical passages.

Having gone through all of these steps, one or more run-throughs should take place, at least for a major witness. A word-for-word, scripted performance is not what we have in mind. Instead, there ought to be a review of the order of the evidence and the important points to be dealt with in each section. Remember, there is nothing improper about reviewing a witness's evidence with that witness before the witness testifies. While there are certain circumstances in which you may not speak to the witness about his or her evidence – for example when a witness you have called in chief is being cross-examined – reviewing a witness's evidence beforehand is not only proper, it is essential. [5]

The frequency with which you will be able to meet with and prepare your witness will vary from case to case and will depend on the complexity of the case and the importance of the witness. As the trial date approaches, however, it is important to again review your witness's evidence with that witness at the latest possible moment before they are to testify. Given the exigencies of the trial and the cost associated with witness preparation, this may not always be possible. Where it is possible, however, you must do it.

A balance must be struck between, on the one hand, maintaining a degree of spontaneity and freshness in the witness's testimony and, on the other, having the witness well enough prepared to be both comfortable and effective. We think it is useful to go through the crucial portions of the evidence using questions in the exact form you will be asking them in court. This will give the witness a chance to become accustomed to the form of the questions. On key material, the witness must know exactly how you will ask the question and have firmly in mind the key points of the answer in a logical order which comprise a complete response.

Finally, the witness must be told to:

---

[5] The professional obligations and ethical limits on communicating with a witness both before and during the course of a proceeding are discussed in greater detail below in Chapter 9, **9.4 Presenting Witnesses**.

(a) speak slowly and clearly;

(b) speak towards the judge;

(c) listen carefully to the question being asked; and

(d) answer the question asked.

(f) Evidence by Way of Witness Statement or Affidavit

In an effort to streamline the evidence-gathering process and reduce costs, some jurisdictions have imposed rules that require certain evidence to be adduced by way of affidavit, rather than by oral testimony. This is particularly the case in applications, motions, and trials for relatively small amounts of money.[6] This is also a feature of many arbitrations, and in certain jurisdictions, virtually all evidence in chief is adduced by what is referred to as a witness statement.[7]

In cases where the evidence is to go in by affidavit, the lawyer must take special care to ensure that the words ring true. It is no easy task to accurately capture another person's story and commit it to paper, but this is exactly the task a lawyer takes on when preparing an affidavit. What must be borne in mind is that, although the drafting is virtually always done by the lawyer, it is ultimately the witness who must swear to, and stand by, the statement's contents. Accordingly, in preparing the affidavit, think carefully about who your witness is and how your witness would relay the facts that comprise the document. Remember, it is the witness, not you, who will be cross-examined on the affidavit, and if the affidavit is drafted using terms that the witness would never use – or worse

---

[6] In Nova Scotia, for example, Rule 53.02 states: "The direct evidence of a witness on a motion or application must be provided through an affidavit, unless a presiding judge permits direct examination." Ontario has in place a "Simplified Rules" regime, with special rules that apply to trials where the sum in dispute is less than $100,000. These "summary trials" are typically short, with evidence in chief being presented by affidavit, followed by oral cross examination. At the other extreme, for Ontario's Commercial List Court, which adjudicates some of Canada's most high-stakes disputes, the Court encourages the use of sworn witness statements to replace examination in chief, in whole or in part, "in appropriate circumstances", see Ontario, Superior Court of Justice, Commercial List, Practice Direction, available online at: http://www.ontariocourts.on.ca/scj/en/notices/pd/toronto/commercial.htm.

[7] In the U.K., until recently, all in chief evidence at Commercial Court trials was adduced by witness statement. In the Eastern Caribbean States, the practice of using witness statements is mandatory for all trials pursuant to Part 29 of the Eastern Caribbean Supreme Court Civil Procedure Rules 2000.

still, does not understand – opposing counsel may exploit the discorrespondence to make it seem like the affidavit is a piece contrived by the lawyer.

When preparing an affidavit, a good practice is simply to have the witness prepare a written narrative statement for you, describing the facts from his or her perspective. Where more information is needed, ask the witness to prepare a supplementary statement on the point that requires elaboration. With these pieces in hand, you will be better able to prepare an affidavit that stays true to the witness's story, and equally importantly, the witness's voice. Insofar as is possible, use the witness's language and turns of phrase, not yours, when transforming the witness's narrative into an affidavit. Your role is to ensure that the affidavit flows well and is easy to read and understand, it is not to put words in the witness's mouth or make him or her swear to a statement with which he or she does not feel comfortable.

When preparing affidavits, you must guard against the problem of the overly deferential witness. A witness may trust your writing or phraseology over his or her own. You must ensure that, by the time the witness is prepared to swear or affirm to the truth of the affidavit's contents, the words on the page are the witness's, not yours. It does your witness no good to agree to a statement, in deference to your perceived drafting skills, only to have that witness resile when the veracity of that statement is tested under cross-examination.

4

PREPARATION FOR CROSS-EXAMINATION

4.1 INTRODUCTION

It is important in our view to prepare the witness for cross-examination by dispelling "the myth". The myth is that cases are won by devastating cross-examination. In truth, cases are won or lost on the facts. The critical job for you as counsel, where you have the opportunity, is to so position the impending case so that the opponent is forced to fight the case on the ground of your choosing. Insofar as is possible, you want to set out the factual context that is most advantageous to your case. In any event, it is in making the witness fully aware of the facts that the best protection for the cross-examination is found.

4.2 SOME BASIC "DO'S" AND "DON'TS"

If the witness has been thoroughly and carefully prepared to give evidence in chief, very little other preparation for cross-examination will be needed. The witness will have arrived at his or her best recollection of the relevant events and will have reviewed all prior statements and testimony. You will have canvassed areas of likely inconsistency and conflict with the witness and determined whether there is anything else that the witness knows which is relevant to the matters in issue in the case. Having done all that, it is wise to acquaint the witness with some of the standard cautions for cross-examination.

There are a number of fairly standard but important cautions that are given to witnesses to prepare them for cross-examination.

- Listen to the question. Make sure you understand the question. If you do not understand it, say so.
- Answer the question asked and none other. Give a complete answer but do not volunteer any information not required by the question.
- Do not concern yourself at all with where the questioning is leading. Concentrate only on the question asked and the giving of an accurate and complete answer.
- Remember the usefulness of the word "but". If a yes or no answer will result in an incomplete answer, the answer "Yes, or no, but (with the qualification)" is an effective riposte.[1]
- Do not guess at an answer. If you do not know the answer, say so.
- Be polite even if it kills you.
- Do not look to the lawyer who has called you as if for help or to see how you are doing.
- Do not let words be put in your mouth. Use your own words. Beware of any false assumption which is rolled into the question. If there are any inaccuracies built into the question, correct them.
- Beware of the two-part question and make sure you respond to both parts appropriately.

---

[1] For example, this type of answer is most effective when dealing with previous testimony or statements. The cross-examiner will put to you that the earlier statement by you was the truth, the inference being that your present and inconsistent answer is false. Your answer may well be "yes" when you made the earlier statement when you believed it to be true, "but" as a result of information since received, you now know it to be wrong.

The following similar points are given by H.H. Spellman in *Direct Examination of Witnesses*: [2]

> (c) The witness should avoid losing his temper or becoming irritated by cross-examining counsel. If he is able to keep his temper, the witness will make an excellent impression on the trier of the facts. If cross-examining counsel addresses unpleasant questions to the witness, such counsel, if the answers of the witness are returned in a dispassionate manner, will probably irritate the fact-finder.
>
> . . . . .
>
> (e) On cross-examination, a witness should do his best to answer "Yes or No" to the cross-examiner's question.
>
> (f) On cross-examination, the witness should avoid the temptation of trying to explain an unfavourable answer necessarily given by him. It should be impressed upon a prospective witness that the easiest way to defeat cross-examination is by answering truthfully and simply, even though the answer may be damaging to the party calling the witness. Sometimes a simple yes or no answer to a cross-examiner's question may be harmful; but the witness should trust the counsel for the party calling him to explore the subject more fully on redirect examination and, thus, to minimize (or indeed, destroy) the apparently harmful effect of a simple affirmative or negative answer to the "trick" question.
>
> (g) A witness should answer all questions he understands. He should not hedge, or stall, or argue with the counsel questioning him. He should not give the impression of being so partisan that his testimony may not be fully believed.
>
> (h) A witness should not try to outguess cross-examining counsel. The cross-examiner has the advantage of knowing where his question will lead. He has planned his tactics and strategy in advance. The witness cannot, in this aspect, be a match for him and should not try to be.

In addition, it is probably wise to discuss with the witness the standard "trick" question: "Have you discussed your evidence with anyone before today?" The witness should be assured that there is nothing at all improper in discussing the evidence beforehand. If asked, the failure to admit discussions with counsel would in itself be an admission of inadequate preparation. The obligation with respect to that question, as well as the other questions, is to tell the truth to the best of the witness's ability.

---

[2]   *Direct Examination of Witnesses* (Englewood Cliffs, N.J.: Prentice-Hall, 1968), at p. 52. Used by permission of the publisher, Prentice Hall/A division of Simon & Schuster, Englewood Cliffs, N.J.

4.3   PREPARING THE FIRST-TIME WITNESS

(a)   Describe the "Ordeal"

The witness must be advised that cross-examination is an "ordeal". For the major witness it will be a test of wills. It is no help to a witness to minimize the experience of cross-examination. The witness who is savaged by a cross-examination and whose integrity is adversely commented on by the judge, will not appreciate the fact that he or she had no idea of the potential risk.

(b)   Do Not "Spook" the Witness

The witness must, however, be reassured that with proper preparation, there is little to fear. Natural apprehension in the prospective witness is to be expected. If properly harnessed, it can motivate a witness to prepare fully. Beware an absence of some nervousness. A confident first-time witness in the early stages of preparation may tell you that you have not adequately explained the "ordeal".

(c)   Insist on Detail

The witness must be advised that only close attention to detail and hard work will do. Make this point early and if necessary make it often. Further, it is no good to expect the witness to prepare on his or her own for the cross-examination. Time must be spent together discussing the documents and probing the facts. Here is where the preparation for the evidence in chief and the cross-examination meet. Complete mastery of the facts by the witness is required.

(d)   Cover with the Witness the Particular Direction from Which the Attack Will Come

The witness will expect to be advised what the cross-examination will canvass. These areas must be covered so that the witness will feel comfortable and able to meet the attack. The usual target for cross-examination will be the evidence adduced in chief. Obvious care will be taken in the preparation to receive this attack. However, a most effective cross-examination may leave the usual target area alone and instead take aim at other areas where the witness has evidence.

Consequently, time must be spent on canvassing those other areas in which the witness's evidence may be helpful to the other side. There is nothing more disconcerting than to watch your witness being led by the nose through areas helpful to the other side and which are news to you. If time permits, a practice cross-examination may be helpful but should not be undertaken at the expense of properly analyzing all the facts and documents in detail. Remember, if your preparation has been thorough, there is no one in a better position than you to cross-examine.

(e)   Advise the Witness that there will be Areas of Attack by Cross-Examination that May Come as a Complete Surprise

The witness must be advised that this is normal and provided he or she has answered your questions in preparation truthfully, there is nothing to fear if the cautions set forth in section 4.2, above, are adhered to.

4.4   PREPARING THE WITNESS WHO HAS BEEN THROUGH IT BEFORE

It is important to ascertain if the witness has had any previous experience giving evidence. If he or she has, then the following is important.

(a)   Find out What the Earlier Case Was and the Witness's Involvement in it

This is important for several reasons. First, you will want to get the transcripts if there is any chance that this witness has previously given testimony on matters relevant to the issues in the current case. Second, you will want to check whether adverse findings of credibility were made in the earlier case in relation to this witness. Third, knowledge of the earlier experience of the witness may assist you in explaining to the witness how the current case will be different.

(b)   Find out What the Witness was Taught about Giving Evidence in the Earlier Case and the Reaction to the Experience

The witness's reaction to the earlier experience will assist you in dealing with specific concerns or anxieties that the witness has as a result of it. The description of what the witness was taught before will also help identify what lessons need to be retaught, reinforced or perhaps erased. You must explain to the witness what your approach is and that you expect your approach to be followed by the witness. If your approach differs from the earlier experience, explain why.

49

Be wary of the witness who thinks he or she has seen it all before. If the cross-examination in the earlier experience was not difficult, you should stress that it may be very difficult this time. The preparation may have to be such as to induce some humility in the overly confident witness.

4.5 PHYSICAL AND MENTAL PREPARATION FOR THE ORDEAL

As stated, you must advise the major witness that the cross-examination will be a test of wills. The witness will need to be physically as well as mentally prepared. This concern will only arise where the witness is expected to spend a lengthy period of time in the witness box. The giving of evidence over time is exhausting. Where this is to be expected, the witness must be so advised. Some witnesses will start exercising in preparation. Others will stockpile sleep. Others will change their personal habits (*e.g.*, reduce drinking) in order to best enable them to handle the mental and physical stress. The lawyer must offer advice in this area and is probably in the best position to do so since the lawyer will also have developed personal methods of stress management. The witness must be cautioned that when he or she becomes tired, the tendency is for the witness to either become testy or start uncritically accepting the facts being put by the cross-examiner. This tendency must be understood and resisted.

4.6 THE HILLS THAT MUST BE HELD

When preparing the major witness, it may be helpful to identify the vital pieces of evidence in the testimony. You may advise the witness that these are the essential "strong points" which must be adhered to no matter how exhausted or confused the witness may become. Drawing again on the battle analogy, these are the hills that must be held. While the witness must be true to the facts, the properly prepared witness will know that some facts are more important than others. These facts cannot be surrendered.

4.7 RE-EXAMINATION

The witness must be told that if an important incorrect, damaging or incomplete answer has been made in cross-examination, you may ask a question to allow the witness to correct the answer or impression at the end of the cross-examination.

When you ask such questions the witness must listen carefully since you cannot indicate what the right answer is in your question, and perhaps using the last reservoirs of strength, the witness must give a complete answer. Remember, the wrong answer in re-examination can be devastating.

Of course the witness can also be trained to deal with mistakes. Key witnesses can be "in the box" for days, or even weeks, at a time, and no matter how well prepared a witness is, errors or miscommunication are to be expected. Tell your witness that if, while giving evidence, he or she makes a mistake, or realizes that an answer was given that is incorrect, it is best to correct the error as soon as possible. The witness should be told that in such circumstances, it is best to wait for an appropriate moment during his or her testimony and to tell the judge or the cross-examiner that an error may have been made in responding to an earlier question. Almost inevitably, the witness will be allowed to correct the mistake. Of course, the witness should realize that this may open him or her up to further lines of questioning. As such, this should only be done to correct true errors. A jittery witness may have a propensity to revisit evidence in order to clarify or amplify an answer that was given earlier. You must insist that the witness not give in to that temptation.

4.8   CONCLUSION

The goal of these points is to achieve a healthy respect in your witness coupled with a quiet confidence for the cross-examination. Also remember that the ability of the witness may allow counsel to be "creative" in this area. Once you have gained some experience, you may decide to set traps for the cross-examiner by leaving certain matters out of the examination-in-chief so as to entice the questioner in cross-examination into dangerous waters where he or she will be met with a well-prepared position and where you can deliver the "coup de grace" in re-examination. However, if it is a critical point, deal with it in chief.

5

EVIDENCE AND TRIAL PROCEDURE: WHAT THE WITNESS NEEDS TO KNOW

5.1 INTRODUCTION

The witness must have some basic knowledge about the rules of evidence and trial procedure. The purpose of this chapter is to offer some advice on what the witness needs to know about these matters.

5.2 GOALS

The goal of orienting the witness to the trial process is not to allow the witness to pass a law school examination or to appear as counsel at a trial. The real goals are much more modest.

First, you want witnesses to have a basic understanding of the role they are being asked to play: where they fit in the process.

Second, the witness needs to know some of the basic "rules of the road". The knowledge acquired about the trial process and the witness's role should help reduce the fear of the unknown and help overcome the anxiety that the prospect of being a witness will probably induce. The information you give to the witness should relate to these goals. If you overdo the detail, you are unlikely to achieve any of the goals and it is quite likely that you will add to, rather than ease, the witness's anxiety and nervousness.

We are not attempting to write a book on evidence or trial procedure, but rather to set out the material for your review with the witness. How the witness is briefed is another question. You may simply relate the information orally. Some lawyers and firms prepare written memoranda on these subjects for distribution to witnesses.[1]

A videotape of a simulated trial is a more ambitious, but effective, educational tool. The goal here is simply to set out what the witness needs to know about the process.

5.3   THE ROLE OF THE WITNESS

There are three aspects of the witness's role that are important and frequently misunderstood. They need to be explained carefully and simply to the witness during preparation.

1. The witness is to give evidence, not make argument. Some witnesses, especially parties or very friendly witnesses, want to argue the case at every opportunity. It is important that they understand the difference between evidence and argument, and that their only job as a witness is to give evidence.

2. The witness, generally speaking, is to testify about facts rather than to give opinions. This is a somewhat complicated but important concept for witnesses. While there is no clear dividing line between fact and opinion, you should stress in most cases that the witness should testify as specifically as possible about what he or she *saw, heard and did,* rather than about what he or she thought, inferred or guessed. Of course, there are many topics about which a witness may give an opinion. If this is relevant in the particular case, these situations should be reviewed.

3. The witness should answer the question, not argue about its propriety. It must be understood that it is the witness's job to answer questions, provided the question is understood and he or she has knowledge responsive to it. It is the lawyer's job to object to improper questions; failure to object is a sign that the question is proper. The witness may ask that the question be repeated or

---

[1]   See Appendix A, Memorandum for Witnesses — Testifying in Court.

indicate that the question is not understood. Otherwise, the question should be answered without comment about the question. The witness must not make speeches or answer more than the question.

5.4 BEFORE BEING CALLED TO THE STAND

You should review with the witness the possibility of an order excluding witnesses. Aside from not being able to be present in court, the witness must understand that the order prevents him or her from discussing the evidence of witnesses who have already testified and from discussing their own evidence once they have testified. You may also wish to give advice and instruction to your witnesses about their conversations with third parties. Ideally, your witnesses will not discuss their evidence or anything else about the case with anyone except you.

Of course, they are under no obligation in this regard, but it is wise to give this advice hoping they will accede to it. Events very significant to the case sometimes take place just outside the courtroom door while the trial is in progress or during the small talk at breaks. Ships are not the only things that loose lips can sink, and your witnesses should be aware of this simple truth.

The witness should be told about rules relating to discussing the evidence once he or she has begun to testify. Although practices differ from one jurisdiction to another, the basic rule is that the witness must not discuss the evidence once given with anyone until the case is over. During the cross-examination, the witness must not talk about the evidence or how the cross-examination is proceeding with anyone. Witnesses must understand these rules and the importance of complying with them.

5.5 THE OATH OR AFFIRMATION

It is a good practice to review the requirement that evidence be given on oath or solemn affirmation. You should ask whether the witness wishes to swear (on the Bible, Old or New Testament, the Koran, etc.) or affirm. A little advance preparation on your part can prevent an awkward moment while the clerk fumbles to find the form of affirmation and the witness begins to feel that he or she has become a problem.

The consequences of taking the oath or affirming should also be discussed. You should briefly review the existence of criminal offences, such as perjury, and note that deliberately giving false evidence under oath is a serious offence. You should also reassure witnesses that it is not an offence to make an honest mistake and that as long as witnesses tell the truth to the best of their ability, there is nothing to fear.

55

5.6 HOW TO ADDRESS PEOPLE IN THE COURTROOM

The judge should be referred to as "Your Honour". Every male lawyer in a courtroom should be called "Sir" or "Mr. _____", and female lawyers are best referred to as "Ms. _____".

5.7 INTERPRETERS

Section 14 of the *Canadian Charter of Rights and Freedoms* entrenches a constitutional right of a party to have proceedings interpreted. Section 14 reads as follows:

> 14. A party or witness in any proceedings who does not understand or speak the language in which the proceedings are conducted or who is deaf has the right to the assistance of an interpreter.

This right, of course, is neither automatic nor absolute. It is available to individuals who demonstrate that they are unable to speak or understand the language in which the proceedings are taking place and provides for competent interpretation. The Supreme Court of Canada, in the leading case of *R. v. Tran*[2] identified the basic standard of interpretation to include an acceptable level of continuity, precision, impartiality, competency and contemporaneousness.

This concept has been incorporated into the rules of procedure of the courts. In Ontario, for example, Rule 53.01 states that

> (5) Where a witness does not understand the language or languages in which the examination is to be conducted or is deaf or mute, a competent and independent interpreter shall, before the witness is called, take an oath or make an affirmation to interpret accurately the administration of the oath or affirmation to the witness, the questions put to the witness and his or her answers.
>
> (6) Where an interpreter is required under subrule (5), the party calling the witness shall provide the interpreter, unless the interpretation is to be from English to French or from French to English and an interpreter is provided by the Ministry of the Attorney General.

Thus, when dealing with a witness who is unable to understand or communicate in the language of the proceedings, it is important for counsel to recognize that interpreters are available to ensure that the individual is able to understand and participate. Counsel must also

---

[2] (1994), 92 C.C.C. (3d) 218, 117 D.L.R. (4th) 7, [1994] 2 S.C.R. 951, 133 N.S.R. (2d) 81, 32 C.R. (4th) 34, 23 C.R.R. (2d) 81, 24 W.C.B. (2d) 308 (S.C.C.).

consider who will be hired to provide interpretation services. In a civil setting, the rules contemplate that the party calling the witness is the party who will arrange for the interpreter. In the criminal context, courts in metropolitan centers retain rosters of qualified interpreters, although it is important to note that not all interpreters are accredited.

Recent cases have turned the spotlight on quality of interpretation, whereby stays of proceedings and mistrials have been declared as a result of shoddy interpretation.[3] Although an accredited interpreter is not required, counsel should nonetheless take steps to ensure that the interpreter being used is able to perform adequately the services being asked of him or her. To this end, an additional safeguard in place is the interpreter's oath, whereby interpreters swear that they understand the language to be interpreted and that they shall accurately interpret to the best of their abilities the proceedings. The precise words of the oath differ from province to province, but the concept is the same: litigants and witnesses are to receive competent interpretation. The proper administration of justice depends on it.

5.8 QUESTIONS FROM THE JUDGE

Questions from the judge should also be discussed. The witness should realize that the judge may ask questions at any time, but the practices of particular judges vary considerably. The witness should not take judicial interrogation as a bad sign, but simply answer the judge's question in a straightforward and truthful way. At the same time, the witness should be cautioned against letting the judge put words in his or her mouth. While deference and politeness to the judge are never misplaced, one should be on guard against acceding too readily to judicial paraphrases or other suggestions from the bench unless they are completely accurate. The temptation to agree with the judge will be great, so the witness must be prepared to politely but accurately recast matters if the judge's words are in any way inaccurate. Questions from the bench may also alert the witness to problems such as speaking too quickly or not being sufficiently clear.

5.9 HEARSAY

The witness needs to be told something about "hearsay".

"Certainly no one save a lawyer can understand the law of evidence, and . . . no lawyer, even though he may admit to understanding that law,

---

[3]   See *R. v. Sidhu* (2005), 203 C.C.C. (3d) 17, 67 W.C.B. (2d) 736 (Ont. S.C.J.) and the cases cited by Justice Casey Hill therein.

could ever explain it."[4] This remark is particularly apt with respect to the rule against hearsay evidence, a rule described as "one of the most complex and most confusing" in the law of evidence.[5] We include these discouraging statements by way of caution. It is hard to make any safe generalizations to witnesses about the hearsay rule, and more importantly, attempts to do so may lead the witness to become unduly concerned about repeating what others have said. It is very dangerous for a witness to become preoccupied with the rules of evidence. The result may range from the witness becoming uncertain and unsettled to failing to concentrate on the key factual matters on which his or her evidence is required. You should be careful not to allow the witness to be too concerned about the hearsay rule.

The best approach is to first give the witness a brief definition and a few examples of evidence excluded by the hearsay rule. You should add, though, that there are many exceptions, even when the rule is being strictly applied and that very often, hearsay evidence is admitted as a matter of convenience. This will alert the witness that legal debates about hearsay may come up, but that it is counsel's worry, not the witness's. Second, your detailed preparation of the witness's evidence in chief should anticipate and deal with any hearsay problems that are likely to arise. In this way, the real problems will be fully dealt with without burdening the witness with a lot of general information about the hearsay rule.

There are a few turns of phrase that may assist a witness to avoid hearsay problems. For example, where there has been a discussion between the witness and others, the witness will probably want to report what each person said in this sort of testimony: "Harry told me, X, then Glenda said". Instead, the witness could testify, avoiding the hearsay problems, as follows: "I discussed the matter with Harry and Glenda and as a result, did X". In other kinds of situations, the passive voice may come in handy. Compare "I went to the doctor and she told me to stay off work for a week", with "I went to the doctor. It was decided that I should stay off work for a week".

---

[4] C.A. Wright, "The Law of Evidence: Present and Future" (1942), 20 Can. Bar Rev. 714 at p. 719.

[5] R. Cross and C. Tapper, *Cross and Tapper on Evidence*, 11th ed. (New York, Oxford University Press, 2007), at p. 587.

5.10   PRIVILEGE

Counsel should also take time to explain issues of privilege to a witness. Specifically, the witness should understand what it means for information or documents to be privileged, and should be warned of the various ways in which privilege may be lost or waived.

Solicitor-client privilege and litigation privilege are two common forms of privilege that are of particular interest for the purposes of this book. Although these are two types of privilege that you will encounter in your practice, there are others, and it is important that you familiarize yourself with the various forms of privilege, preferably before you prepare your witnesses and certainly before you enter the courtroom.

Solicitor-client privilege is the privilege that attaches to communications between the client and the lawyer. These communications are considered to be confidential and the privilege that attaches to them is absolute in scope and permanent in duration. The functional purpose of solicitor-client privilege has been said to go to the very heart of the administration of the legal system. As Mr. Justice David Corbett recently summarized the doctrine:

> The functional purpose of solicitor-client privilege goes to the very heart of the administration of the legal system. All persons, whether natural, corporate, or governmental, must have access to expert legal counsel without fear that this recourse may be used to their detriment: *Jones* v. *Smith* at S.C.R. 474-475; *Gruenke* at S.C.R. 289. Solicitor-client privilege is a "fundamental civil and legal right" (*Solosky*, at S.C.R. 839) and is "fundamental to the justice system in Canada" (*R.* v. *McClure*, 2001 SCC 14 (CanLII), [2001] 1 S.C.R. 445, per Major J.).
>
> . . . . .
>
> The general statement of the principle in Wigmore still stands as a reasonable summary, in the following terms (*Pritchard* (C.A.) at O.R. 104-105):
>
>> Where legal advice of any kind is sought from a professional legal advisor in [his or her] capacity as such, the communications relating to the purpose made in confidence by the client are at [its] instance permanently protected from disclosures by [the client] or by the legal advisor; except that the protection be waived.[6]

Of course solicitor-client privilege will only apply when the person with whom you are communicating is your client. When dealing with

---

[6]   *Guelph (City)* v. *Super Blue Box Recycling Corp.*, 2004 CanLII 34954, 2 C.P.C. (6th) 276, [2004] O.J. No. 4468, 134 A.C.W.S. (3d) 787 (Ont. S.C.J.).

third parties, such as other witnesses or potential witnesses, litigation privilege may apply so as to protect communications, notes, memoranda, and other information obtained or created in the litigation context. The Supreme Court of Canada decision in *Blank v. Canada (Minister of Justice)*[7] is the leading authority in distinguishing litigation privilege from solicitor-client privilege, and defining the former's limits:

> The solicitor-client privilege has been firmly entrenched for centuries. It recognizes that the justice system depends for its vitality on full, free and frank communication between those who need legal advice and those who are best able to provide it. Society has entrusted to lawyers the task of advancing their clients' cases with the skill and expertise available only to those who are trained in the law. They alone can discharge these duties effectively, but only if those who depend on them for counsel may consult with them in confidence. The resulting confidential relationship between solicitor and client is a necessary and essential condition of the effective administration of justice.
>
> Litigation privilege, on the other hand, is not directed at, still less, restricted to, communications between solicitor and client. It contemplates, as well, communications between a solicitor and third parties or, in the case of an unrepresented litigant, between the litigant and third parties. Its object is to ensure the efficacy of the adversarial process and not to promote the solicitor-client relationship. And to achieve this purpose, parties to litigation, represented or not, must be left to prepare their contending positions in private, without adversarial interference and without fear of premature disclosure.[8]

This "zone of privacy" around materials related to the preparation for litigation is not as absolute as the privilege that attaches to communications between lawyer and client. It expires once the litigation has ended, and can also be set aside on a *prima facie* showing of actionable misconduct on the part of a party in relation to the proceedings with respect to which the litigation privilege is claimed.[9]

It is difficult to overemphasize the importance of having a grasp over the issue of privilege. The above summary is merely the starting point. Public interest privilege, informer privilege, and doctor patient con-

---

[7]   [2006] 2 S.C.R. 319, 270 D.L.R. (4th) 257, 51 C.P.R. (4th) 1, 47 Admin. L.R. (4th) 84 *sub nom.* Blank v. Canada (Department of Justice), 40 C.R. (6th) 1, 2006 CarswellNat 2704, [2006] S.C.J. No. 39, 2006 SCC 39, 352 N.R. 201, 150 A.C.W.S. (3d) 401.

[8]   *Supra*, at paras. 26-7.

[9]   *Supra*, at paras. 34 and 45.

fidentiality are other forms of privilege that should also be considered in the appropriate cases.

Further, especially when dealing with witnesses or litigation in foreign jurisdictions, you must ensure that you understand any differences that may apply. For example, under the U.S. Federal Rules of Evidence, information that is shared with a witness in preparation for testimony, or while testifying, is potentially discoverable pursuant to Rule 612 if the document was presented to the witness so as to refresh his or her memory. In such a case, the opposing party is entitled to production and to cross-examine the witness on the document. As such, U.S. counsel are at times very cautious in terms of the materials they will present to a witness in preparing that witness to give evidence, the concern being that any document that a witness reviews may be construed as having refreshed the witness's memory. For example, a chronology prepared by a lawyer for the purposes of assisting a witness to remember a sequence of events may well be producible under these rules. Such a document, which might otherwise be protected by the U.S. form of "work-product privilege", may lose its protected status and become open to inspection.[10] In Canada, by contrast, although documents such as the witness's notes or prior statements used to refresh a witness's memory can be the subject of a production order, solicitor-client and litigation privilege have thus far proven robust enough to ensure that, where a lawyer shares with a client or a third party materials prepared for litigation, the communication will remain privileged.[11]

In preparing your witness, you should explain notions of privilege and must identify for the witness how privilege may be lost. Importantly, the concept of waiver of privilege must be described, so as to make the witness aware that if he or she voluntarily discloses privileged informa-

---

[10] For a useful discussion of these forms of privilege in the U.S. context, see "Interactions Between Memory Refreshment Doctrine and Work Product Protection Under the Federal Rules", Note (1978), 88 Yale L.J. 390.

[11] None of the leading Canadian authorities cite cases of a lawyer's work product being disclosable simply because it was shown to a witness in the course of preparing for trial. Our own research has also not turned up cases that would run contrary to the general principle that communications between a lawyer and a third party, the dominant purpose of which is preparation for litigation, are protected by litigation privilege. See, *e.g.*, Alan W. Bryant, Sidney L. Lederman, and Michelle K. Fuerst, *Sopinka, Lederman & Bryant: The Law of Evidence in Canada*, 3d ed. (Markham: LexisNexis, 2009), at §14.178-§14.198 and §16.111, for a discussion of litigation privilege and production of documents used to refresh a witness's memory, respectively.

tion in the course of giving evidence, the door may be open to opposing counsel to probe further and to obtain information and documentation that might otherwise have been cloaked in privilege. You, as prudent counsel, should identify potential trouble spots for the witness in advance, and forewarn the witness that if he or she is asked a question that could lead to a waiver of privilege, you will rise to object to the question.

5.11   OBJECTION TO QUESTIONS

We have already mentioned that it is for the lawyers, not the witnesses, to object to improper questions. However, it is important for witnesses to understand what they should do when an objection is raised. Your advice to the witness on this subject can be quite simple.

1. The witness should be aware that counsel may make objections. If you are objecting to a question asked in cross-examination, you will be trying to prevent improper questioning. If the opponent objects during the evidence in chief, the purpose may be to avoid specific damaging testimony or to generally unsettle the witness.

2. The witness must know enough to stop talking as soon as counsel begins to object. There is nothing more disheartening than making your objection while the witness completes the answer.

3. The witness should remain calm and collected and appear completely disinterested in the legal squabbling. No concern should arise if the witness is excused from the courtroom while the objection is argued. You should reassure the witness that this is normal procedure.

4. The witness should not speak again until spoken to. Either the judge will ask the witness to answer or counsel will repeat the question.

5.12   CONCLUSION

We have touched on the points that we think witnesses should be made aware of concerning trial procedure and evidence. The challenge is to cover this material so that it reduces, instead of enhances, anxiety. In general, we think that you should convey to the witness that you, the lawyer, are being paid to worry about the rules of evidence. The witness is there to give testimony about what happened. The orientation that we propose is to make the courtroom somewhat less unfamiliar and to assist witnesses to present their testimony in a straightforward manner, concentrating on the facts, not the process.

6

PREPARATION FOR EXAMINATION FOR DISCOVERY

6.1 THE IMPORTANCE OF PREPARATION FOR DISCOVERY

Many more cases proceed through discovery than are litigated to the end of the trial. This fact alone suggests that effective discovery preparation is a vital part of counsel's arsenal. For practical purposes, the discovery will often be the final step in the action before it is settled or otherwise disposed of. The discovery may be the only occasion on which one of your key witnesses, your client, will actually testify.

Recently, in an attempt to rein in the costs of litigation, Ontario amended its rules to place time limits on examinations for discovery. Now, regardless of the number of parties or persons to be examined, no party may examine for discovery for more than seven hours except with the consent of the parties or with a court order. This decrease in time should in no way be understood to diminish the importance of examination for discovery. If anything, your witness needs to be even more prepared so as to ensure that the discovery process unfolds smoothly and efficiently.

The discovery experience is an important part of client preparation to testify at the trial. The discovery may be the witness's first experience testifying under oath and it will probably be the first exposure to the experience of being questioned by the opponent's counsel. It may also be your first opportunity to assess how the witness performs in this setting, and the opponent's questioning may reveal new information about the other side's case, their views of the facts, and strategy. For all of these reasons, the preparation for discovery should be taken just as seriously as the preparation for trial itself.

6.2   EXPLAINING THE PROCESS OF DISCOVERY TO THE WITNESS

At the outset, the witness must understand both the institutional and the tactical purposes of discovery. On the institutional side, the objective of providing disclosure that will assist preparation for trial, narrow the issues, and perhaps facilitate settlement, should be explained. With respect to tactics, a full explanation of some points will have to be given.

First, the witness must understand that it is important to provide opponents with the sort of discovery to which they are entitled under the rules. Failure to do so may not only add needlessly to the expense and delay of the litigation, but may, in extreme cases, lead to the imposition of sanctions or, more importantly, the drawing of adverse inferences at trial. Second, the witness must understand that their own discovery is not designed to help their case. In general, the less said beyond what the opponent is entitled to and asks about the better. Third, the witness must understand the uses to which the transcript of the examination may be put. For example, the witness may be cross-examined on the discovery transcript if there is some inconsistency between the testimony at trial and the earlier evidence on discovery or the discovery evidence may be read in by the opponent as proof of elements of the case.

In explaining to the witness how a transcript from discovery is used, it may be of assistance to show a witness a transcript from another discovery you have conducted (after satisfying yourself about any confidentiality concerns). This can be used to illustrate for the witness the need to provide succinct, responsive answers. Longwinded answers that span pages of transcript merely open the witness up to potential cross-examination and impeachment at trial. Further, showing the witness the transcript provides a clear illustration that a transcript is "neutral". That is to say, tone, humour, and sarcasm do not translate well onto the page. Finally, this exercise can be used to show a witness that answers such as "um hum" or "uh huh" are poor, and potentially harmful, proxies for "yes" or "no", and can lead to ambiguity or confusion down the road.

All of this is by way of caution that the informal atmosphere which often prevails at discovery should not mislead the witness as to the importance or seriousness of the process. Finally, the witness should know that the opponent will be assessing the strength of the witness's case and the performance of the witness as a witness. If the witness performs well at the discovery, the likelihood of a reasonable settlement may increase.

6.3 PREPARATION FOR TESTIMONY AT DISCOVERY: HOW IT DIFFERS FROM PREPARATION FOR TESTIMONY AT TRIAL

In some aspects, there is no difference in principle between the preparation for testimony at trial and the preparation for testimony on discovery. The record will not be as complete at the discovery stage because you will not have the transcripts of the examinations of the other parties at this point and you will not have the additional productions that almost always emerge for the first time during the oral examination and thereafter. However, the factual investigation and review with the witness must be as intense and complete as possible. At a minimum, this must include review of the pleadings, the productions, and any other available documentation. The witness's narrative should be reviewed for completeness, consistency with the other known facts, and inherent probability. Rough spots should be reviewed. All of this is identical to the sort of fact investigation and witness preparation that we advocate for trial purposes.

There are, however, some important differences between preparation for discovery and preparation for trial. Most of them flow from the different scope of discovery examination, the different rules of admissibility of evidence, and the different tactical purposes which are in play at discovery.

As is well known, most rules governing discovery in common law Canada require the witness to answer questions concerning relevant matters to the best of his or her "knowledge, recollection, information and belief". This, of course, means that the witness is not confined to answering from first-hand knowledge, as generally will be the case at trial, but must answer to the extent of his or her knowledge, information and belief. In addition, the witness has a duty to become informed in various ways so that the result of these inquiries may be relayed to the opponent. One major aspect of preparation for discovery testimony is effective handling of this wide obligation to report second-hand information.

In general, there are two important techniques to respond to this obligation. First, all second-hand information should be checked and double-checked before it is reported. Sometimes, busy executives or entrepreneurs, for example, will make their inquiries too hastily or interpret the responses too uncritically. The result may be inaccurate information that will have to be corrected later and may cause problems for the case. You, as counsel, should ensure that the inquiries have been properly conducted and make reasonable efforts to verify the information.

The second technique comes into play at the discovery itself. During the examination, it is important to identify those parts of the testimony that are based on second-hand evidence and to introduce whatever qualifications are appropriate with respect to that information. For example, in an appropriate case, the witness might say something to the effect that this is the best obtainable information, but that he or she is not able to vouch for the accuracy of the information personally. Different considerations come into play when a witness is being examined as the representative of a corporate party, so that even answers based on second-hand information may be binding on the party.

6.4   DISCOVERY PREPARATION: OTHER MATTERS

(a)   Admissions

The opponent will be seeking admissions at the discovery.

As part of the preparation, you should assess what admissions should properly be made. The exact scope and wording of any admissions should be carefully reviewed so that the proper admission, but no more, will be made.

(b)   Style of Questioning

The witness on discovery must be ready to deal with a broad range of styles of questions. Some examiners tend toward broad, general questions which attempt to put the onus on the witness to provide the relevant information. The witness's counsel will, of course, object to overly general questions. The witness, however, must be able to provide a coherent account of the relevant matters in response to fairly general questions. As a rule, broad, general questions should elicit short, general answers. For example:

Q. Describe the events of the evening of June 16, 1990.

A. I was driving north on West Street and was involved in a collision, was injured and taken to hospital.

This answer is an appropriate one to the question, but puts the onus on the examiner to ask more specific questions.

Some examiners will cross-examine. The same basic approaches to preparation for cross-examination come into play as discussed in Chapter 5. The witness and counsel must take special care with the assumptions and conclusions imbedded in the questions put on discovery. Such assumptions may be legal, factual or both, and it is important that no ground be given unwittingly as a result of failure to recognize them in the questions. For example:

Q. I am sure you weren't paying attention to the time, but can you give an estimate of the time this happened?

A. 8:30.

At trial, if the opponent's contention is that the incident happened earlier, this answer may be put to the witness to show that he or she was not paying attention to the time and can only give an estimate. A better answer, assuming the facts support it, would be:

A. In fact I was paying attention to the time and know that it was at 8:30.

Beware the "friendly" examiner. Perhaps the most dangerous examiner is the one who makes the witness relax and become conversational. The witness must be told to answer only the question. Nothing is to be volunteered. The silence at the end of an answer is golden and not to be filled with further words.

(c) Reviewing the Pleadings

A common technique on discovery is for the examining counsel to place the witness's pleading before him or her and to go through each paragraph asking what facts are relied on in support of the particular allegation. This technique should be reviewed with the witness so that he or she is able to respond appropriately.

(d) Taking Counsel's Directions During the Examination

A major difference between discovery and trial is the ability of the witness's counsel to intervene to answer questions or refuse to answer questions. The possibility of this sort of intervention should be reviewed with the witness so that it will not take the witness by surprise. The witness should also be told to take counsel's directions no matter what. Faced with a refusal to answer, some opponents may try to bully the client into answering or adopt other rather unprofessional techniques. These sorts of tactics should be discussed with the witness in advance, and the importance of following counsel's instructions reviewed. Further, you should forewarn the witness that while he or she is being discovered, you will not be discussing evidence that has been given to date.

(e) After the Discovery Examination

As soon as the transcripts are ready, both counsel and the witness should review them for errors and inaccuracies. There is an obligation to advise the opponent of these matters and it is wise to do so.

6.5 A CLIENT MEMO TO AID PREPARATION

One useful vehicle for preparation is a written memorandum about the discovery process which can be given to the client and studied at leisure. We include an example as Appendix B, Examination for Discovery.

7

PREPARING EXPERTS

7.1 INTRODUCTION

Justice Stephen Goudge, in his Commissioner's "Inquiry into Pediatric Pathology in Ontario", recently noted the following:

> [T]he legal system, as a general rule, prohibits witnesses from testifying about their opinions, as opposed to facts they have observed. It is the trier of fact who must draw conclusions based on the evidence presented at trial. Expert witnesses are allowed to give opinion evidence as an exception to the general rule, but only to the extent that they have been properly qualified as experts.[1]

In working with expert witnesses, it is important to keep the expert's role squarely in mind and remember that experts serve a special function. The expert is not meant to usurp the role of the trier of fact, nor is the expert meant to be an advocate for the client or act as a "hired gun". Rather, the expert is to provide objective, neutral assistance to the court by providing an independent opinion about technical matters that are likely to be outside range of experience of the trier of fact. This specialized role requires counsel to take special care to ensure that the expert fulfils that role with a due level of objectivity and skill.

---

[1] Ontario, *Inquiry into Pediatric Forensic Pathology in Ontario, Report: Policy and Recommendations*, vol. 3 (Toronto: Queen's Printer, 2008), at p. 471 ["Goudge Report"].

An "expert" witness plays a unique and important role in a trial, as the expert is permitted to testify as to inferences, the drawing of which requires special skill, training and experience. Dickson J. (as he then was) described the expert's role as follows:

> An expert's function is precisely this: to provide the judge and jury with a ready-made inference which the judge and jury, due to the technical nature of the facts, are unable to formulate. "An expert's opinion is admissible to furnish the Court with scientific information which is likely to be outside the experience and knowledge of a judge or jury. If on the proven facts a judge or jury can form their own conclusions without help, then the opinion of the expert is unnecessary." (*R. v. Turner* (1974), 60 Cr. App. R. 80 at p. 83, per Lawton L.J.)[2]

An expert may play three roles — first, to provide advice to assist your fact investigation or your examination of opposing experts; second, an expert may be called as a witness; and third, the expert may be used to comment on the reports and opinions of other experts, both yours and your opponents'. Our discussion concentrates on experts you will be calling as witnesses, but two broader points are worth making here. You should keep in mind the role of the particular expert as you deal with him or her. This relates specifically to the issue of what aspects of the expert's work are open to discovery. In addition, do not avoid experts whose opinions are unfavourable to your case. They may be very useful to you in preparation of the experts you intend to call, particularly in ensuring that you have anticipated and dealt with all possible lines of attack, as well as preparing you for the experts you will have to cross-examine.

Many of the things we have said about preparing witnesses in general also apply to expert witnesses, but there are some features of the expert as a witness that give rise to special considerations. These are:

(a) you will likely be able to choose the expert;

---

[2] *R. v. Abbey* (1982), 138 D.L.R. (3d) 202 at p. 217, 68 C.C.C. (2d) 394, [1982] 2 S.C.R. 24, 43 N.R. 30, [1983] 1 W.W.R. 251, 29 C.R. (3d) 193, 39 B.C.L.R. 201. For advice on all aspects of expert witnesses, see Robert B. White, Q.C., *The Art of Using Expert Evidence* (Aurora: Canada Law Book, 1997) and Glenn R. Anderson, *Expert Evidence*, 2nd edition (Markham: LexisNexis Canada, 2009). Mark J. Freiman and Mark L. Berenblut, *The Litigator's Guide to Expert Witnesses* (Aurora: Canada Law Book, 1997) and K.M. Matthews, *et al.*, *The Expert: A Practitioner's Guide* (Toronto: Carswell, 1995), contain discussions of particular types of experts. For a discussion of the role of the expert in the criminal law setting, see Alan D. Gold, *Expert Evidence in Criminal Law: The Scientific Approach* (Toronto: Irwin Law, 2003).

(b)   the expert will be testifying as to opinions rather than facts;

(c)   the expert will often testify as to the factual basis of the opinion, even if this would otherwise be hearsay. The expert will also be relying on current professional knowledge which comes in hearsay form; and

(d)   the expert usually will have conducted investigations or tests and will be presenting a written report.

7.2   RETAINER

The three key elements concerning the retainer of the expert witness are:

(i)   the choice of the expert;

(ii)   the scope and purpose of the retainer; and

(iii) the co-ordination of experts.

The witnesses who "saw it happen" are selected by fate. However, in many instances, the experts who will testify for your client are selected by you. Although this is a bit of an over-generalization, the opportunity to select your expert is an important step in successful preparation.

The threshold consideration is qualification. The key point is whether the witness has acquired special skill and knowledge through education and/or experience that permits the drawing of inferences from the facts which would be difficult or impossible for the layperson to draw. The more direct the link between the witness's training and experience and the particular issues with which he or she will deal, the more qualified the witness is. The next factor is that of "believability". This is a very subjective factor reflecting qualifications, ability to speak and write clearly, skill in presenting complex material in an understandable and effective way, and ability to deal successfully with cross-examination.

The best way to judge these matters is by reviewing previous reports filed by the witness, reviewing any judicial comments about the witness in previous cases and polling colleagues who have had experience with the witness.

7.3   THE DUTY OF THE EXPERT CALLED AS A WITNESS

Insofar as testifying experts are concerned, it is essential that you be clear about the scope and purpose of the retainer and ensure that the expert understands the role of the expert in the court room. In his recent report titled *Civil Justice Reform in Ontario*, the Hon. Coulter Osborne identified the need to emphasize that an expert is meant to be independent and impartial:

> The issue of "hired guns" and "opinions for sale" was repeatedly identified as a problem during consultations. To help curb expert bias, there does not appear to be any sound policy reason why the Rules of Civil Procedure should not expressly impose on experts an overriding duty to the court, rather than to the parties who pay or instruct them. The primary criticism of such an approach is that, without a clear enforcement mechanism, it may have no significant impact on experts unduly swayed by the parties who retain them.
>
> An expressly prescribed overriding duty to provide the court with a true and complete professional opinion will, at minimum, cause experts to pause and consider the content of their reports and the extent to which their opinions may have been subjected to subtle or overt pressures. Matched with a certification requirement in the expert's report, it will reinforce the fact that expert evidence is intended to assist the court with its neutral evaluation of issues. At the end of the day, such a reform cannot hurt the process and will hopefully help limit the extent of expert bias.[3]

These findings resulted in amendments to Ontario's Rules of Civil Procedure, whereby a testifying expert's duty is now expressly articulated as follows:

DUTY OF EXPERT

4.1.01(1) It is the duty of every expert engaged by or on behalf of a party to provide evidence in relation to a proceeding under these rules:

    (a) to provide opinion evidence that is fair, objective and non-partisan;

    (b) to provide opinion evidence that is related only to matters that are within the expert's area of expertise; and

    (c) to provide such additional assistance as the court may reasonably require to determine a matter in issue.

Duty Prevails

(2) The duty in subrule (1) prevails over any obligation owed by the expert to the party by whom or on whose behalf he or she is engaged.[4]

The need for independence and impartiality is difficult to overstate. Recently, there has been an increased focus on discouraging using experts as advocates. As stated at the outset of this chapter, the expert owes an overriding duty to assist objectively the court. Although the expert is

---

[3]   Coulter A. Osborne, Q.C., *Civil Justice Reform Project: Summary of Findings and Recommendations* (Ontario Ministry of the Attorney General, 2007), at pp. 75-6, available online at: http://www.attorneygeneral.jus.gov.on.ca/english/about/pubs/cjrp/CJRP-Report_EN.pdf.

[4]   *Rules of Civil Procedure*, R.R.O. 1990, Reg. 194.

retained by a party, it is important that the expert not see him or herself as acting as that party's advocate. Conflating the expert's role with that of the advocate risks the tainting of the expert, such that a court may dismiss an expert as being biased or unreliable. An expert may come to identify or sympathize with your client's case, but when the identification or sympathy is such that it clouds the expert's ability to independently and impartially draw conclusions from facts and assumptions, that witness will be seen to have crossed the line.[5]

Another issue to consider from the outset is discoverability. Experts who are to be called to testify may well have to produce all their background material and drafts, whereas this will not occur when an expert simply advises you on issues in the case, but is not called to testify.[6] When dealing with experts, you should constantly keep in mind whether their work will be discoverable; this will turn to a great extent on whether they will be testifying or not.

The scope of discoverability of a testifying expert's file is matter of some controversy, although in recent years, the trend in the jurisprudence has been toward greater transparency and disclosure. In British Columbia, there has been since at least 1987 jurisprudence that supports the proposition that, when an expert is to be called as a witness, there is an implied waiver of any privilege that might otherwise have applied to his or her work product.[7] In recent years, the same notion has gained acceptance in Ontario as well, most notably in Justice Eileen Gillese's chambers' decision in *Horodynsky Farms Inc. v. Zeneca Corp.*[8] There, Justice Gillese held that drafts of experts' reports could be the subject of a production order, as the drafts represent preliminary findings, opinions, and conclusions that an opposing party should be entitled to test.[9]

---

[5] See, for example, *Piersanti v. Alfano* (2009), 78 C.P.C. (6th) 88 *sub nom. Carmen Alfano Family Trust v. Piersanti*, [2009] O.J. No. 1224, [2009] CanLII 12799, 176 A.C.W.S. (3d) 152 (Ont. S.C.J.).

[6] In Ontario, see Rule 31.06(3), which expressly shields a party from having to disclose information or material relating to an expert that the party undertakes not to call as a witness at trial.

[7] *Vancouver Community College v. Phillips, Barratt* (1987), 20 B.C.L.R. (2d) 289, 27 C.L.R. 11, 38 L.C.R. 30, 7 A.C.W.S. (3d) 138 (S.C.).

[8] (2006), 272 D.L.R. (4th) 532, 82 O.R. (3d) 229, 214 O.A.C. 161, *sub nom. Conceicao Farms Inc. v. Zeneca Corp.*, [2006] O.J. No. 3012, 150 A.C.W.S. (3d) 316 (C.A.).

[9] A three-judge panel later set aside Gillese J.A.'s order on other grounds: (2006), 272 D.L.R. (4th) 545, 83 O.R. (3d) 792, 215 O.A.C. 233, *sub nom. Conceicao Farms Inc. et al. v. Zeneca Corp.*, 32 C.P.C. (6th) 201, 2006 CarswellOnt 5672, [2006] O.J. No. 3716, 151 A.C.W.S. (3d) 567 (Ont.

This trend has expanded to encompass the production of e-mails between counsel and the expert, or the expert and the client, the expert's notes of any meetings or discussions regarding the preparation of the report, and all documents which could reasonably be seen to have been foundational to the preparation of the expert's report.[10] As such, a great deal of care must be taken by counsel in communications involving the expert.

In preparing your expert, you must work from the presumption that the entirety of the expert's file will make it into the opposing party's hands. Written communications with an expert must therefore always be professional, judicious, and reflect an understanding of the expert's role and duties. If communications come to light that can be seen as encouraging the expert to act as your client's advocate, rather than as an impartial participant, your expert's credibility may be brought into question under cross-examination.

Many cases now involve more than one expert and frequently their evidence is interrelated. For example, in a municipal planning case, you may require the evidence of a zoning expert or planner to establish the highest and best use of a site, an architect to say what can be built on the site and an appraiser to say what the site is worth. Each witness contributes a piece of the whole and relies on the others for the basis of their own work. Co-ordination is essential if the total presentation is to be effective; it is a factor that should be considered at the outset. In choosing experts, counsel should assess their capacity to work together, and make clear to each the interrelated aspects of the work. It may also be possible to place some of the co-ordinating responsibility on one of the experts.

7.4   QUALIFICATIONS

Nothing is more important than the expert's qualifications. Of course, the admissibility of expert testimony depends in part on the witness's

---

C.A.), leave to appeal to S.C.C. refused 275 D.L.R. (4th) vii, [2007] 1 S.C.R. viii, 233 O.A.C. 396*n*, 367 N.R. 399*n*, *sub nom. Conceicao Farms Inc. v. Zeneca Corp.*

[10] See, for example, *Aviaco International Leasing, Inc. v. Boeing Canada Inc.*, [2002] O.J. No. 3799, 117 A.C.W.S. (3d) 51 (Ont. S.C.J.); *Browne (Litigation Guardian of) v. Lavery* (2002), 58 O.R. (3d) 49, 37 C.C.L.I. (3d) 86, 18 C.P.C. (5th) 241, [2002] O.J. No. 564, 111 A.C.W.S. (3d) 1103 (Ont. S.C.J.); *Ramer Builders Supplies (Toronto) Ltd. v. Leva*, [2009] O.J. No. 592, 174 A.C.W.S. (3d) 998 (Ont. S.C.J.). For a full discussion of this trend, see Richard H. Shekter, "Current Issues in Expert Evidence", Presentation to the Advocates' Society Spring Symposium 2009 (May 8, 2009).

qualifications. It is useful to recall the four criteria for the admissibility of expert evidence set out by the Supreme Court of Canada in *R. v. Mohan*:[11]

    (i)   relevance;
    (ii) necessity in assisting the trier of fact;
    (iii) the absence of any exclusionary rule; and
    (iv) proper qualifications.

Recently, there has been renewed interest in the so-called gatekeeping role that judges are to play in ensuring that the admission of expert evidence is reliable and will further the fact-finding exercise. While threshold reliability was once seen as being relegated to areas of "novel science", jurisprudence is now trending toward testing all expert evidence against a standard threshold of reliability.[12] As Justice Ian Binnie held, in a case that has since been taken up by lawyers and judges calling for increased scrutiny over the admissibility of expert evidence:

> In the course of *Mohan* and other judgments, the Court has emphasized that the trial judge should take seriously the role of "gatekeeper". The admissibility of the expert evidence should be scrutinized at the time it is proffered, and not allowed too easy an entry on the basis that all of the frailties can go at the end of the day to weight rather than admissibility.
>
> The Court's gatekeeper function must afford the parties the opportunity to put forward the most complete evidentiary record consistent with the rules of evidence . . .
>
> Nevertheless, the search for truth excludes expert evidence which may distort the fact-finding process.[13]

Counsel must therefore prepare the witness to define clearly the discipline regarding which the expert evidence is being proffered and the precise scope of the witness's expertise. As well, counsel must be prepared (and must prepare the witness) to defend the reliability of the scientific theory or technique upon which the expert's opinion is based. You may also have to address whether the theories being relied upon are generally accepted or disputed within the discipline, and whether they have been subjected to meaningful peer review.

---

[11] (1994), 114 D.L.R. (4th) 419, [1994] 2 S.C.R. 9, 18 O.R. (3d) 160*n*, 71 O.A.C. 241, 29 C.R. (4th) 243, 89 C.C.C. (3d) 402, 166 N.R. 245.

[12] Goudge Report, *supra*, footnote 1, vol. 3, at p. 480.

[13] *R. v. J. (J.-L.)* (2000), 192 D.L.R. (4th) 416, [2000] 2 S.C.R. 600, 148 C.C.C. (3d) 487, 37 C.R. (5th) 203, [2000] S.C.J. No. 52, 2000 SCC 51, 261 N.R. 111, 47 W.C.B. (2d) 591. See also Shekter's discussion of this case, *supra*, footnote 10.

All of the above factors can affect the judge's determination as to threshold reliability. To this end, it will generally be insufficient to merely demonstrate to the court that the witness has specific expertise in a recognized discipline. Where the expert, as is usually the case, will be giving opinion evidence, the witness must be able to articulate how his or her qualifications relate specifically to the questions on which the opinion will be sought. You should be able to articulate precisely the matters on which the opinion will be asked, and relate the expert's qualifications directly and specifically to those matters.

Finally, you must prepare the witness to respond to the above queries even in the absence of an objection by opposing counsel. In the Goudge Report, it was noted that the absence of an objection should figure prominently in a judge's decision to embark on an intensive examination of threshold reliability. Nonetheless, the Commissioner noted, "[T]he trial judge retains the responsibility of determining the admissibility of expert scientific evidence, regardless of the absence of an objection from counsel."[14] As such, it is wise to prepare your expert to withstand whatever scrutiny that the trial judge may bring to bear in exercising the gate-keeping function with respect to expert evidence.

Of course, the qualifications are important far beyond the issue of the admissibility of the proposed evidence. The qualifications are a vital part of the witness's "believability". A few practical points to consider on the issue are:

1. Don't succumb to blind faith in formal education. While formal credentials are often important, real-life experience is often equally or more important. An experienced truck driver may be a more convincing expert on some issues than a hydraulic engineer. Practical know-how may be very important. Think carefully about the precise issues that need expert help and then consider whether there is someone whose job relates to them on a daily basis. That person may not have all the degrees, but may make an excellent expert witness.

2. When considering the expert's education, consider also his or her participation (whether as a student or instructor) in continuing education initiatives. Such participation will help emphasize that the expert is knowledgeable and up to date on developments in the discipline.

---

[14] Goudge Report, *supra*, footnote 1, at p. 496.

3. Don't stop at the standard form resumé. Many expert witnesses have detailed, standard form resumés. They may omit or skip over things important to your particular case. Probe these things and have them developed and emphasized in the resumé to be used in your case.

4. Watch out for puffery. A padded resumé is dangerous. Review all the claims made on the resumé in detail and consider having a knowledgeable person in the relevant field review and comment on it.

5. Specific examples of other retainers may be helpful. If the expert has worked on some impressive projects, make sure these are described.

6. Judicial comments and reviews of books are helpful. If a court in reasons for judgment commends an expert or a review praises something he or she wrote, these comments may make a useful addition. Conversely, if a judge has previously questioned, or worse still, criticized an expert's candour or reliability, you should be very cautious about relying on that expert to help support your case.

7. Beware the professional witness. People who make a living as witnesses may have very impressive qualifications. But the fact that they make their living as witnesses may detract from their believability. A successful professional life outside the courts is a real asset for an expert witness.

7.5 THE FACTS

An expert will usually have two jobs relative to the facts:

(i) obtaining facts through investigation or tests; and
(ii) drawing inferences from those facts as well as from facts testified to by other witnesses.

Nothing is more important to the effectiveness of the expert's testimony than a sound factual basis. One of the standard techniques of cross-examination of an expert is to show that the facts relied on are either incorrect or incomplete. Great care must be taken in this area. Some key points are:

1. The expert must be aware of all of the relevant facts in the case. You must give the expert all relevant material, good and bad, and where facts are disputed, instruct the expert as to the facts to be assumed for the purposes of the analysis.

2. Review every factual assumption the expert makes and check it against the primary sources (i.e., transcripts, exhibits, witness statements, etc.).

3. Make sure all factual elements that must be proved, will be proved. The law as to which factual aspects of the expert's opinion must be proved is somewhat unpredictable, but you should deal with these points as part of your preparation.

4. As early as possible, develop a sense of the key facts from the expert's point of view. Early knowledge of this will help at discovery as well as assist other fact investigation.

7.6 PREPARATION OF REPORTS

In almost all civil matters, counsel will have to provide the opponent with a written report in advance of calling an expert at trial. The filing of the report has several consequences:

(a) the privilege relating to the expert is waived;
(b) the other side has time to review the report carefully and have other experts comment on it;
(c) the report may go in as evidence without oral evidence being called;
(d) the witness may be cross-examined and, in some jurisdictions, discovered on the report; and
(e) the expert will have to commit himself or herself to a view of the facts and to an opinion.

All of these factors speak to the importance of the expert's report. Accordingly, the report warrants as much or more care as the oral evidence. As well, it is important to review the rules of procedure pertaining to experts' reports. For example, the Rules of Civil Procedure in Ontario set out certain specifications to which an expert's report must adhere; these are set forth below:

> 53.03 (2.1) A report provided for the purposes of subrule (1) or (2) shall contain the following information:
>   1. The expert's name, address and area of expertise.
>   2. The expert's qualifications and employment and educational experiences in his or her area of expertise.
>   3. The instructions provided to the expert in relation to the proceeding.
>   4. The nature of the opinion being sought and each issue in the proceeding to which the opinion relates.

5. The expert's opinion respecting each issue and, where there is a range of opinions given, a summary of the range and the reasons for the expert's own opinion within that range.
6. The expert's reasons for his or her opinion, including,
    i.   a description of the factual assumptions on which the opinion is based,
    ii. a description of any research conducted by the expert that led him or her to form the opinion, and
    iii. a list of every document, if any, relied on by the expert in forming the opinion.
7. An acknowledgement of expert's duty (Form 53) signed by the expert.[15]

The signed acknowledgment set out in point 7 above constitutes a particularly important development. The acknowledgement relates back to Rule 4.1.01, which we discussed earlier in this chapter. Having the expert sign an acknowledgement of the expert's duty is meant to further emphasize for the expert the need for him or her to execute responsibly the task of providing opinion evidence that is fair, objective and non-partisan. The acknowledgement is simply one more device being developed by the courts in seeking to enhance their gatekeeping function and ensure that testifying experts are not used as "hired-guns" in the trial process.

The following are some of the points that should be considered in the preparation of the expert's report:

1. Define the task precisely. The expert should be able to say exactly what he or she has been asked to do in a few simple sentences. If the scope is limited in a particular way, the limitation should be clear and sensible. It is usually best for counsel to prepare a letter setting out the expert's assignment. The lawyer should anticipate that the letter of instructions will be produced at trial.

2. When to move to the first draft. How early in the process the witness should begin to commit his or her ideas to paper will vary from case to case. The report of the family physician in a routine personal injury case will probably be obtained right away. The report of a forensic accountant in a complex breach of trust case may be a very different matter. In some cases, counsel may not want the expert to begin writing until after the opponent's discovery. In any case, we suggest that no drafts be done until counsel is sure that the expert understands the assignment, has enough of the necessary factual information, and it appears likely that the opinion will be of use to the client. You should operate on the assumption that drafts

---

[15] Rules of Civil Procedure, R.R.O. 1990, Reg. 194.

will have to be produced if the witness testifies. We suggest that counsel and the expert agree on the outline that the report will follow and discuss the key conclusions in advance of the first draft.

3. You must emphasize that you want the expert's unbiased professional opinion. This must be explicitly at the foundation of your relationship for both ethical and tactical reasons.

4. Reviewing draft reports:

   (a) The language should be as simple as possible, expressing the technical material in layperson's language. The structure of the report should be logical and comply with the relevant rules of court as to form and content.

   (b) The discussion must be detailed enough that the conclusions flow from the premises. Detail and supporting data should be put in appendices, so as not to detract from the flow and force of the report.

   (c) Visual aids should be used liberally. Simple diagrams, pictures, charts, etc., can greatly aid understanding of complex material.

   (d) The report must have a clear conclusion which sums up the report and states the opinion(s) in a few simple sentences. Unnecessary qualifiers, limitations, etc., should be deleted.

   (e) Check the report for internal consistency, for consistency with the other evidence, and with anything the expert has written on the subject. You should review any reports on related topics or published work authored by the expert (or his or her firm). Many experts also publish books and articles which can provide your opponent with rich material for cross-examination. These problem areas should be detected and dealt with sooner rather than later.

   (f) Put aside the detail and ask whether the essence of the report makes sense. Counsel should be able to express the essence of the report in a few simple sentences. If this is not possible, the case needs much more work (or much less!).

   (g) Assess the expert's "comfort level" with the report. Is the expert overstating the opinion or trying too hard to please? These are the early warning signs of expert self-destruction. Heed them.

   (h) Make sure the prospective witness, not an assistant, is on top of the material.

Many experts rely heavily on assistants to carry out some of the work and to author reports. This may not be problematic in itself. You need to make sure that your witness, not the assistant, will be able to testify knowledgeably and confidently.

7.7 EVIDENCE IN CHIEF

As with any witness, the fundamental question with an expert is how does the evidence relate to the matters that must be proven. With all of the technical details and subissues that can arise with expert evidence, it is important not to lose sight of this basic objective. Another fundamental point relates to the use of language. The same words may have quite different meanings in law than they do in other disciplines, and the same sort of complication may exist among other disciplines. Causation is one thing to a social scientist and another to a lawyer. In preparing the witness to testify, these problems of language must be reviewed and addressed.

Generally in civil matters, a report will have to be filed before the evidence is called and the report may be entered as an exhibit. If the report has been carefully done, preparation for the examination-in-chief should be relatively easy. The form of the report should be followed and the witness should not be afraid to read key conclusions from it *verbatim* if it is made an exhibit.

The following points are also suggested:

1. The oral evidence about qualifications should expand on the written resumé. Make sure the expert is ready to do this in the areas you think important.

2. The oral evidence may go into considerably more detail about the background and methodology than does the report. The expert should describe the discipline or subject of expertise as well as the techniques he or she has brought to bear on the problem.

3. The evidence in chief should address specific points raised by the opponent's experts. It can be effective to prepare exhibits containing the key parts of the other side's expert's reports along side a summary of your expert's answer or comment.

4. Consider the use of large charts or other aids. It may be effective to enlarge some of the tables from the report for use at trial. It is always nice to have a key element of your case sitting on the easel for all to see throughout the trial.

5. The expert must not become an advocate. Your preparation must stress that the expert's professional opinion is all that is desired. The testimony must be fair-minded and unbiased.

Melvin Kraft included a helpful checklist in *Using Experts in Civil Cases.*[16] Some of his most important points are:

1. Be sure the expert is completely objective and truly impartial, rather than serving as a surrogate advocate.
2. Be sure the expert avoids inserting himself into the case, as by communicating with the adverse party, his counsel, or his expert or other witnesses.
3. Be sure the expert avoids any references to the personalities of litigants or of counsel.
4. The fee of the expert should be no more than commensurate with the time and effort expended in the particular case, the difficulty of the case, and the expert's professional charges.

 . . . . .

6. The attorney calling the witness should carefully review the records of the witness's prior professional association and engagements, and seek to learn his peers' evaluation of the competence of the witness.
7. The witness's prior experience as an expert witness should be explored and the number and types of the litigation should be accurately ascertained, and prior opinion testimony scrutinized.
8. He should be cautioned to avoid any public comment, above all to the press, radio, TV or other publicity media.
9. Any and all books or articles written by the witness . . . should be carefully reviewed for inconsistencies with the witness's proposed testimony at the future trial.

7.8   HYPOTHETICAL QUESTIONS

The hypothetical question is a device to make clear which facts the expert is assuming to exist for the purposes of the opinion. The advantage of this style of question is that it helps make the factual assumptions quite clear. The disadvantages are that a hypothetical question will be much too long if the facts are complicated and, further, that this form of question does not help differentiate the important facts from the unimportant facts. It is not essential to use hypothetical questions. A simple technique is to have the witness review the key facts on which the opinion is based. If hypothetical questions are to be used, they should be written out in full and carefully reviewed with the expert. The written question can then be marked as an exhibit at trial. The casting of the hypothetical question should not be left to be done while the expert waits in the witness box.

---

[16]   (New York: Practising Law Institute, 1977), at pp. 32-33. Reprinted with permission of the Practising Law Institute (New York City).

7.9   PREPARATION FOR CROSS-EXAMINATION

If the report and the evidence in chief have been carefully prepared, little will remain to do for cross-examination. Ideally, you should have a separate expert advising you on the potential weak areas of your witness's report and testimony. At the very least, you can compare your report with that of the other side and with any standard texts in the field. All the usual advice to witnesses about cross-examination holds true for experts, but a few points are particularly important:

1. The expert must not become combative, defensive or appear as an adversary during cross-examination.
2. Beware the attempt to have the expert speculate about the facts. If certain facts have been assumed, the expert should simply say so and not speculate about what may or may not have happened.
3. Beware the textbook. You should review the technique of cross-examination on a textbook with the witness. Witnesses should be careful about acknowledging a book as authoritative and always insist on seeing the context in which a passage appears.
4. The expert should readily state that he has been paid but only at his usual professional rates.
5. The expert must beware of the factual assumptions embedded in the question. If an answer turns on the existence of a particular fact that is assumed by the question, the expert should highlight that distinction at the outset of the answer.
6. If asked to do calculations for example, while testifying, the witness should only do so if this can be done reliably under courtroom conditions. The witness should not agree with figures or any other information that has not been calculated or checked personally.
7. The expert must not become an advocate.

8

PREPARING CHILD WITNESSES

8.1 INTRODUCTION

The subject of child witnesses is a study in itself. It is an area that involves not only legal rules, procedures and tactics, but also issues relating to the science of perception and memory.

The purpose of this chapter is not to provide a detailed review and assessment of the extensive literature or a comprehensive discussion of these matters. Rather it provides an overview of the subject and highlights recent legislative changes which, in many jurisdictions, have overtaken the traditional common law approach to child witnesses.

It is helpful to begin with a brief discussion of witness competence, as this is essential context for several aspects of the discussion which follows. McLachlin J. writing for a majority of the Supreme Court of Canada, summarized the principles relating to witness competence in *R. v. Marquard*:[1]

> Testimonial competence comprehends: (1) the capacity to observe (including interpretation); (2) the capacity to recollect; and (3) the capacity to communicate. The judge must satisfy him-or herself that the witness possesses these capacities. Is the witness capable of observing what was

---

[1]   (1993), 108 D.L.R. (4th) 47, [1993] 4 S.C.R. 223, 66 O.A.C. 161, 85 C.C.C. (3d) 193, 25 C.R. (4th) 1, 159 N.R. 81.

happening? Is he or she capable of remembering what he or she observes? Can he or she communicate what he or she remembers? The goal is not to ensure that the evidence is credible, but only to assure that it meets the minimum threshold of being receivable. The enquiry is into capacity to perceive, recollect and communicate, not whether the witness actually perceived, recollects and can communicate about the events in question.[2]

L'Heureux-Dubé J., writing in partial dissent, took issue with the above characterization, holding that the inquiry into admissibility should focus on the witness's ability to communicate, not perceive and recollect. As will be seen below, recent statutory amendments are consistent with L'Heureux-Dubé J.'s approach, facilitating the receipt of testimony from child witnesses. These amendments highlight the need for counsel to be familiar with the applicable statutory rules before preparing for a case involving child witnesses.

8.2   CHILD WITNESSES: THE LEGAL FRAMEWORK

In order to best prepare child witnesses to give testimony, it is important to grasp the rules regarding the admissibility of children's evidence. The preparation of the child witness is intimately connected to the legal framework which regulates the conditions under which the child's evidence may be received, the manner in which the evidence will be received, and whether there is any alternative to the child giving oral evidence in court. Each of these matters influences the decision to call the witness or not, and the approach to preparation. What follows is a brief review of the legal rules, to help place these issues in their proper context.

(a)   The Competence of Child Witnesses

The general rule is that the evidence of witnesses must be received on oath, or, where permitted by statute, under solemn affirmation or a promise to tell the truth. Historically, children's evidence was viewed with suspicion and treated as unreliable. Presumptively, children were considered to lack the capacity to give reliable testimony. At common law, the question of whether a child could testify was primarily the question of whether the child understood the nature and consequences of taking an oath. In most Canadian provinces, statutory provisions regarding child witnesses had generally tracked this aspect of the common law, requiring the evidence to be given on oath so long as the

---

[2]   *Supra*, at p. 236 [S.C.R.].

child understood the nature of an oath.[3] This concept had been applied to confirm the child's understanding of the moral obligation to tell the truth.[4] If the child understood, the presumption against capacity was dislodged, and the evidence was received; if not, the evidence was rejected.

As is further described below, the past two decades have seen a relaxing of the rules so as to allow for the easier receipt of evidence from children. For example, the legislation now in place in Ontario allows a court to receive a child's unsworn evidence, even if the child does not understand the nature of an oath (*i.e.*, that an oath imposes a moral obligation to tell the truth), but understands "what it means to tell the truth and promises to tell the truth".[5] Other provinces have enacted similar amendments, but require that unsworn evidence from children be corroborated.[6]

Given the Federal Government's constitutional competence over criminal law, the federal practice with respect to children's evidence warrants special consideration. There too, the past 20 years have seen significant developments.

In the federal sphere, the changes began in 1988, in response to concerns of under-reporting of child abuse. At that time, the federal legislation regarding children's evidence was amended to facilitate the receipt of evidence from children, and to allow for the use of testimonial aids such as videotaped statements and screens. Under s. 16 of the *Canada Evidence Act*,[7] the challenging party was not required to satisfy the court that there was an issue as to the capacity of the proposed witness if the child was under 14; the presumption of incapacity was still codified. If the witness understood the nature of the oath and could communicate the evidence, the witness testified under oath or affirmation. If the witness did not understand the nature of an oath but was able to communicate the evidence, the testimony could be received upon the witness's promise to tell the truth. As is the case under Ontario's *Evidence Act*, the federal

---

[3]   See, for example, *Evidence Act*, R.S.O. 1990, c. E.23, s. 18.1 [*Evidence Act (Ontario)*].

[4]   See generally S. Casey Hill *et al.*, *McWilliams' Canadian Criminal Evidence*, 4th ed. (Aurora: Canada Law Book, 2010), at 17:20.30. See also Ron Delisle, Don Stuart and David Tanovich, *Evidence: Principles and Problems*, 8th ed. (Scarborough: ThomsonCarswell, 2007), at p. 435.

[5]   *Evidence Act (Ontario)*, s. 18.1(2).

[6]   Although this requirement for corroboration has been repealed in some jurisdictions, such as Ontario.

[7]   R.S.C. 1985, c. C-5.

legislation repealed the requirement of corroboration for unsworn evidence.

Despite the 1988 amendments, concerns remained about how child witnesses were treated in the justice system. As Epstein J. (as she then was) would later describe:

> The case law considering s. 16 from 1988 to the present [2005] amendments revealed that some children were not giving evidence because of a failure to satisfy the tests set out in s. 16. Children who could not explain the concepts of an oath or a promise to the satisfaction of the court were found not competent to testify even though they appeared able to understand and respond to questions.[8]

In 2005, Parliament made significant changes to the *Canada Evidence Act* in regard to the receipt of evidence of children under the age of 14. As certain commentators put it, the amendments came as a result of "substantial concerns about the treatment of vulnerable persons in the justice system, and the difficulty in prosecuting cases in which they are witnesses".[9] These changes have drastically changed the approach to the competence of child witnesses. Pursuant to s. 16.1 of the *Canada Evidence Act*, children under 14 years of age are now presumed to be competent and are not required – or permitted, for that matter – to take an oath.[10] Absent a successful challenge, their evidence is *prima facie* admissible on the promise to tell the truth.

The amendment has completely reversed the historical approach to the evidence of child witnesses and adopts the approach for admissibility favoured by L'Heureux-Dubé J. in her dissent in *R v. Marquard*,[11] in which she held the court should inquire as to the child's ability to communicate, not the child's ability to perceive, recollect *and* communicate.

The *Canada Evidence Act* now provides:

---

[8]   *R. v. Persaud*, [2007] O.J. No. 432, 151 C.R.R. (2d) 245 (Ont. S.C.J.), at para. 21.

[9]   Nicholas Bala, Katherine Duvall-Antonacopoulos, R.C.L. Lindsay, Kang Lee and Victoria Talwar, "Bill C-2: A New Law for Canada's Child Witnesses" (2005), 32 C.R. (6th) 48 at pp. 49-50 [Bill C-2].

[10]   *Canada Evidence Act, supra,* footnote 7, s. 16.1(1) and (6).

[11]   *Supra,* footnote 1. See also the discussion of the British Columbia Court of Appeal in *R. v. S. (J.)* (2008), 315 D.L.R. (4th) 24, 238 C.C.C. (3d) 522, 61 C.R. (6th) 282, 181 C.R.R. (2d) *sub nom. R. v. S. (J.Z.),* 80 W.C.B. (2d) 773, 2008 BCCA 401, at para. 25, affd 315 D.L.R. (4th) 21, 251 C.C.C. (3d) 1, 2010 SCC 1, 87 W.C.B. (2d) 31.

16.1 (1) A person under fourteen years of age is presumed to have the capacity to testify.

(2) A proposed witness under fourteen years of age shall not take an oath or make a solemn affirmation despite a provision of any Act that requires an oath or a solemn affirmation.

(3) The evidence of a proposed witness under fourteen years of age shall be received if they are able to understand and respond to questions.

(4) A party who challenges the capacity of a proposed witness under fourteen years of age has the burden of satisfying the court that there is an issue as to the capacity of the proposed witness to understand and respond to questions.

(5) If the court is satisfied that there is an issue as to the capacity of a proposed witness under fourteen years of age to understand and respond to questions, it shall, before permitting them to give evidence, conduct an inquiry to determine whether they are able to understand and respond to questions.

(6) The court shall, before permitting a proposed witness under fourteen years of age to give evidence, require them to promise to tell the truth.

(7) No proposed witness under fourteen years of age shall be asked any questions regarding their understanding of the nature of the promise to tell the truth for the purpose of determining whether their evidence shall be received by the court.

(8) For greater certainty, if the evidence of a witness under fourteen years of age is received by the court, it shall have the same effect as if it were taken under oath.

The most drastic change under s. 16.1 is that child witnesses under 14 are now presumed to have the capacity to testify, in contrast to the former s. 16 which presumed the child's capacity to testify was at issue. The child witness is now presumed to be competent and any inquiry into capacity to testify focuses only on the child's ability to understand and respond to questions, not the child's understanding of the nature of truth-telling.

In order to challenge the capacity of a proposed child witness under the new amendments, the challenging party bears the burden of satisfying the court that the child's ability to understand and respond to questions is in issue. This inquiry focuses on the child's basic cognitive and language abilities and the judge must determine whether the child is able to understand and respond to questions.[12] If the child is not found to be capable of testifying, "this may be a ground for establishing the 'necessity' for the admission of hearsay evidence instead of having the

---

[12] Bill C-2, *supra*, footnote 9, at p. 54.

child testify".[13] The test for hearsay evidence in the case of children will be discussed later in this chapter.

Section 16.1(2) expressly prohibits witnesses under 14 from taking an oath or making a solemn affirmation, even if it is required by another statute. Children are only required to promise to tell the truth before they may give evidence. Under the previous legislation, counsel and the court could question a child about the child's understanding of what it means to tell the truth. Now, although a child can be questioned about the meaning of truth-telling during the trial phase, the child cannot be questioned along those lines at an earlier stage to determine the admissibility of the child's evidence. As such, while a child's understanding as to what it means to tell the truth may ultimately affect the weight of the child's evidence, it cannot be used to affect admissibility.[14] Finally, when the testimony of a child witness is received by the court, the promise to tell the truth is considered to have the same effect of an oath.[15]

Section 16.1 has survived constitutional scrutiny. In *R v. S. (J.)*,[16] a father convicted of sexually assaulting his children brought an appeal challenging the constitutional validity of, among other things, s. 16.1. The accused argued that these provisions violated his ss. 7 and 11(*d*) Charter rights, as the amendments did not adequately ensure the truthfulness of the child witnesses. Smith J.A., for the British Columbia Court of Appeal, upheld the amendments, holding that, pursuant to the new provisions, a child witness will only be subject to a pre-testimonial inquiry if the court is satisfied that the child's capacity to testify is an issue. In those cases, the inquiry will be limited to questions about the ability to understand and respond to questions.[17] The court in *R. v. S. (J.)* went on to state:

> I do not accept the appellant's argument that if a moral obligation to tell the truth is not established, the testimony of the witness should be inadmissible. Parliament, in enacting s. 16.1, has decided that a promise to tell the truth is sufficient to engage the child witness's moral obligation to tell the truth. Section 16.1 places child witnesses on a more equal footing to adult witnesses by presuming testimonial competence. A child witness's moral commitment to tell the truth, their understanding of the nature of a promise to tell the truth, and their cognitive ability to answer questions about "truth" and "lies" may still be challenged on cross-examination during their testimony; their

---

[13] *Ibid.*
[14] See *R. v. S. (J.)*, *supra,* footnote 11, at paras. 23 and 53.
[15] *Canada Evidence Act, supra,* footnote 7, s. 16.1(8).
[16] *Supra,* footnote 11.
[17] *Supra,* footnote 11, at para. 49.

credibility and reliability may still be challenged in the same manner as an adult's testimony may be challenged. These potential concerns, however, go to the weight of the evidence, not its admissibility.[18]

Where the common law and previous legislation was concerned with the admissibility of a child witness's evidence, the new s. 16.1 focuses on reliability. The court was satisfied that a child's promise to tell the truth was a sufficient basis upon which to receive evidence. The court rejected the proposition that the presumed testimonial incompetence of children constituted a fundamental principle of fairness or that presumptive competence diminished an accused's right to a fair trial. Further, the court noted that traditional safeguards are still in place, including the right to cross-examine the witness.[19]

The constitutional validity of s. 16.1 was also challenged in *R. v. Persaud.*[20] In this case, Epstein J. (as she was then) found that the provision did not violate the accused's right to a fair trial or ss. 7 and 11(*d*) Charter rights. The court held that the accused's rights were not impaired by the prohibition on asking the child about his understanding of the nature of an oath because the accused "has no 'vested right' in the evidentiary or procedural rules regarding testimony".[21] As was the case in British Columbia, the court in Ontario held that concerns regarding the child's testimony go to the weight given to the evidence, not to its admissibility.[22] Epstein J. also considered how the court would handle the new provision in jury trials:

> While we no longer consider the evidence of a child to be inherently frail or unreliable (*R. v. W.(R.)* (1992), 74 C.C.C. (3d) 134 (SCC)) the evidence of children must be treated with caution when the circumstances arise. Caution may, for example, be necessary when a very young witness testifies about events that happened much earlier in time or has limited verbal skills. We regularly caution juries to keep in mind the child's ability to observe and remember what happened. We ask them to consider the child's ability to understand the questions and give truthful and accurate answers. We remind juries that young witnesses do not always have the same ability as adults to recall precise details or to describe events fully and accurately.
>
> As a result of the recent amendments to s. 16 of the *CEA* the jury will be in a position to consider, based on the child's evidence, any apparent

---

[18] *Supra*, footnote 11, at para. 52.
[19] *Supra*, footnote 11, at para. 55.
[20] *R. v. Persaud*, [2007] O.J. No. 432, 151 C.R.R. (2d) 245 (Ont. S.C.J.).
[21] *Supra*, at paras. 43-44.
[22] *Supra*, at para. 43.

lack of knowledge of the concepts of truth and falsity and the duty to speak the truth. In the end, the trier of fact may well decide that the child's evidence is of little weight. As we say, "it will be for the jury to decide".

In my view, where the child's evidence has been successfully challenged in cross-examination either in the sense that he or she did not know the difference between truth or falsehood or that he or she did not know the importance of telling the truth, the trial judge can instruct himself or herself or can explain clearly to the jury, in such a way that they will govern themselves in accordance with the directions of the judge, that the child's testimony should be given little or no weight. I do not feel that one must proceed on the assumption that jurors are incapable of understanding instructions of this type or of acting in accordance with them. If such were the case there would be no justification for the existence of juries.[23]

Provincial legislation has not been modified quite as starkly as the federal Act. An example is Ontario's *Evidence Act,*[24] which presumes that children are competent witnesses, but maintains many of the restrictions that have since been legislated away in the *Canada Evidence Act*:

18.1 (1) When the competence of a proposed witness who is a person under the age of 14 is challenged, the court may admit the person's evidence if the person is able to communicate the evidence, understands the nature of an oath or solemn affirmation and testifies under oath or solemn affirmation.

(2) The court may admit the person's evidence, if the person is able to communicate the evidence, even though the person does not understand the nature of an oath or solemn affirmation, if the person understands what it means to tell the truth and promises to tell the truth.

(3) If the court is of the opinion that the person's evidence is sufficiently reliable, the court has discretion to admit it, if the person is able to communicate the evidence, even if the person understands neither the nature of an oath or solemn affirmation nor what it means to tell the truth.

Thus, much like s. 16.1(6) of the *Canada Evidence Act*, a promise to tell the truth can be sufficient to receive the evidence of a child witness. However, in contrast to the federal statute, Ontario's *Evidence Act* still requires a child witness to understand what it *means* to tell the truth. Importantly, however, the court retains a discretion to receive testimony even when this criterion is not met, so long as the court is satisfied that the

---

[23] *Supra*, at paras. 47-49.
[24] R.S.O. 1990, c. E.23.

evidence is sufficiently reliable.[25]

(b) Manner of Giving Evidence

Generally, the child witness will testify in open court although the judge may have the discretion to exclude the public while the child is testifying. In certain circumstances, legislation provides other options, such as allowing the child to give evidence from behind a screen. More precisely, the *Criminal Code* states that, "the judge or justice shall, on application of the prosecutor . . . order that the witness testify outside the court room or behind a screen or other device that would allow the witness not to see the accused".[26] In deciding whether to allow for special manners of giving evidence, the court will consider the age of the witness, whether he or she has any mental or physical disability, the nature of the offence and the nature of the relationship between the accused and the witness.[27]

Similarly, the court may order that a support person of the child's choice be permitted to be present and close to a testifying child,[28] and may prohibit an accused from personally cross-examining a child witness.[29] As well, "a video recording made within a reasonable time after the alleged offence, in which the victim or witness describes the acts complained of, is admissible in evidence if the victim or witness, while testifying, adopts the contents of the video recording".[30]

In addition to these specific provisions, the law respecting hearsay statements by children has developed to the point where, in some situations at least, the child may not be required to testify because the evidence may be admissible in hearsay form through another witness. The leading case in this area is *R. v. Khan*.[31] At a sexual assault trial, the

---

[25] *Ibid.*, s. 18.1(3). British Columbia, Alberta, Saskatchewan, Manitoba and Nova Scotia have followed Ontario's model. These provinces allow for an inquiry to be conducted to determine whether a witness under fourteen understands the nature of an oath and is able to communicate the evidence.

[26] *Criminal Code*, R.S.C. 1985, c. C-46, s. 486.2(1) [*Criminal Code*]. Similar provisions may be found in some provincial evidence statutes: see, for example, *Evidence Act (Ontario)*, s. 18.4.

[27] *Criminal Code, ibid.*, s. 486.1(3).

[28] *Ibid.*, s. 486.1. See also *Evidence Act* (Ontario), s. 18.5.

[29] *Criminal Code, ibid.*, s. 486.3. In such circumstances, the court may appoint counsel to conduct the cross-examination. See also *Evidence Act (Ontario)*, s. 18.6.

[30] *Criminal Code, ibid.*, s. 715.1; see also *Evidence Act (Ontario)*, s. 18.3.

[31] [1990] 2 S.C.R. 531, 59 C.C.C. (3d) 92, 41 O.A.C. 353, 79 C.R. (3d) 1, [1990] S.C.J. No. 81, 113 N.R. 53, 11 W.C.B. (2d) 10 [*Khan*]. See also *R. v. Rockey*,

Crown sought to adduce a statement by the three and one-half year old alleged victim to her mother about one-half hour after the incident. The Supreme Court of Canada held that "hearsay evidence of a child's statement on crimes committed against the child should be received, provided that the guarantees of reliability and necessity are met".[32] With respect to the requirements of necessity and reliability, the court held:

> Necessity . . . must be interpreted as "reasonably necessary". The inadmissibility of the child's evidence might be one basis for a finding of necessity. But sound evidence based on psychological assessments that testimony in court might be traumatic for the child or harm the child might also serve.
>
> The next question should be whether the evidence is reliable. Many considerations such as timing, demeanour, the personality of the child, the intelligence and understanding of the child, and the absence of any reason to expect fabrication in the statement may be relevant on the issue of reliability.[33]

The necessity requirement was considered in detail in *R. v. F. (W.J.)*,[34] where McLachlin J. (as she then was), writing for the majority, held that extrinsic evidence is not essential for a finding of necessity. While there must be a foundation for the trial judge's ruling on the question of necessity, that foundation:

> . . . may arise either from the facts and circumstances of the case as revealed to the trial judge, or from [the] evidence . . . Where what occurs at trial satisfies the judge that there is no reasonable prospect of obtaining a meaningful account of the events from the child by direct evidence, the judge may well find necessity on the basis that it is self-evident.[35]

This brief review of the law has important implications for the preparation of a child witness:

* The threshold question is whether the child will be permitted to testify. Under s. 16.1 of the *Canada Evidence Act*, witnesses under 14 are presumed to be competent and must only promise to tell the truth. Pursuant to certain provincial evidence legislation, an inquiry

---

[1996] 3 S.C.R. 829, 140 D.L.R. (4th) 503, 110 C.C.C. (3d) 481, 30 O.R. (3d) 577n, 95 O.A.C. 134, 2 C.R. (5th) 301, 204 N.R. 214, 32 W.C.B. (2d) 339.

[32] *Khan, supra*, at p. 548.

[33] *Supra*, at pp. 546-7.

[34] [1999] 3 S.C.R. 569, 178 D.L.R. (4th) 53, 138 C.C.C. (3d) 1, [1999] 12 W.W.R. 587, 180 Sask. R. 161, 27 C.R. (5th) 169, 247 N.R. 62, 205 W.A.C. 161, 43 W.C.B. (2d) 471.

[35] *Supra*, at p. 590.

may be permitted to probe a child's understanding of what it means to tell the truth.

- A second question is whether the child's testimony may not be essential because the evidence may be given in hearsay form through another witness. Here the statutory provisions and common law developments will have to be considered. A key consideration is the impact on the child of testifying. Counsel should pay special attention to this issue and consider obtaining expert opinion on the question. An example of such expert opinion is detailed in the *Rockey* case, referred to earlier.

- A third question arises if the child is to testify. Is it possible to make special arrangements for the testimony to make the experience less potentially traumatic for the child?

Once again, the relevant statutory provisions, as well as the inherent authority of the trial judge, must be considered. For example, may the child's evidence in chief be given by the child simply adopting a videotaped statement? May the trial judge direct the evidence be given using a screen or closed-circuit television? May members of the public be excluded during the testimony? May the evidence be given in another setting altogether such as the child's home or some other familiar place? May counsel both agree to have the child called by the judge to give evidence so that the child does not believe he or she is choosing sides? This is especially important in family disputes.

These are some of the issues that should be addressed as part of the preparation. Once again, great weight should be given to the welfare of the potential child witness. The various options are only as available as the determination of counsel to take advantage of them.

8.3 PARTICULAR CONCERNS WITH CHILDREN'S EVIDENCE

The common law restrictions on the evidence of children were spawned by concern that children's evidence was inherently unreliable. While early research into the question supported this traditional view, more recent studies have put to rest many of the doubts that fostered that broad scepticism of children's testimony.[36] It is safe to say that courts

---

[36] For a review of the early research, see Gail S. Goodman, "Children's Testimony in Historical Perspective" (1984), 40 Journal of Social Issues 9. There are many detailed sources which discuss the research into children's evidence and its implications for practice. Examples include: H. Dent and R. Finn, eds., *Children as Witnesses* (Chichester: John Wiley and Sons, 1992);

have now unequivocally rejected the notion that children's evidence is inherently unreliable.[37] Nonetheless, preparing a child witness raises particular challenges, and some issues warrant particular attention. We highlight below some concerns about children's evidence that counsel would be wise to consider and address when preparing children for testimony.

(a) Memory

In general terms, current research holds that children do not remember as well as adults, but that information provided through a child's free recollection is generally accurate, especially about core elements of an experience.[38] While a child's memory improves as the child gets older, children as young as four are able to provide an accurate description of an event that happened up to two years prior.[39] That said, research also suggests that there is an acute danger of loss of detail over time. In one

---

L.S. McGough, *Child Witnesses: Fragile Voices in the American Legal System* (New Haven: Yale University Press, 1994); Poole and Lamb, *Investigative Interviews of Children* (American Psychological Association, 1998).

[37] See, for example, *R. v. W. (R.)*, [1992] 2 S.C.R. 122, 74 C.C.C. (3d) 134, 54 O.A.C. 164, 13 C.R. (4th) 257, [1992] S.C.J. No. 56, 137 N.R. 214, 16 W.C.B. (2d) 304. For a comprehensive view on current judicial perceptions of children's testimony, see Nicholas Bala, Karuna Ramakrishnan, Roderick Lindsay and Kang Lee, "Judicial Assessment of the Credibility of Child Witnesses" (2004-2005), 42 Alta. L. Rev. 995 at p. 999 [Judicial Assessment].

[38] See Ralph Underwager and Hollida Wakefield, *The Real World of Child Interrogations* (Springfield, Ill.: Charles C. Thomas, 1990), at p. 28; M. Johnson and M. Foley, "Differentiating Fact from Fiction: The Reliability of Children's Memory" (1984), 40 Journal of Social Issues 33. For more recent writing on this topic, see also Helen L. Westcott, "Child Witness Testimony: What Do We Know and Where Are We Going?" in Belinda Brooks-Gordon and Michael Freeman, eds., *Law and Psychology* (New York: Oxford University Press, Inc., 2006), at p. 204; Erna Olafson, "Children's Memory and Suggestibility" in Kathleen Coulborn Faller, ed., *Interviewing Children About Sexual Abuse: Controversies and Best Practices* (New York: Oxford University Press, Inc., 2007), at p. 18; Michael E. Lamb, Irit Hershkowitz, Yael Orbach & Philip W. Esplin, *Tell Me What Happened: Structured Investigative Interviews of Child Victims and Witnesses* (West Sussex: John Wiley & Sons Ltd., 2008), at pp. 24-6; Nicholas Bala, Katherine Duvall-Antonacopoulos, R.C.L. Lindsay, Kang Lee and Victoria Talwar, "Bill C-2: A New Law for Canada's Child Witnesses" (2005), 32 C.R. (6th) 48 at p. 49.

[39] Carole Peterson, "Children's Long-term Memory for Autobiographical

---

case, for example, an account given by the child 14 days after the incident was found to be much more detailed and realistic than one given six and one-half months later.[40] This suggests that prompt interviewing and recording of accounts is particularly important in the case of children.

Research also suggests that children's recollections tend to be more accurate in reference to core elements of an experience, as compared to peripheral details.[41] This should be borne in mind when assessing the accuracy or veracity of a child's account of an event, as it would be a mistake to discount a child's story simply because some of the more peripheral – and possibly less relevant – details are less consistently recounted.

(b)   Suggestibility

Research in the area has consistently held that children are more prone to suggestions made by the interviewer or others. Underwager and Wakefield summarize the matter as follows:

> . . . recent studies have found young children to be more suggestible than adults and younger children to be more suggestible than older children . . . Young children are particularly bad at making eyewitness identifications, especially when the target individual is not present in the lineup. In such cases, the child makes a very large number of false identifications . . .
>
> . . . . .
>
> . . . [certain studies] indicate that the young children's suggestibility could be partially accounted for because that they are especially likely to conform to what they believe to be the expectations of the adult.[42]

Other research confirms that leading questions are likely to elicit inaccurate information from children, in part due to a propensity on the part of young children to be responsive, even when they may not understand the question being asked of them. The result is that in such circumstances, young children will tend to answer yes/no questions in the

---

Events" (2002) 22 Developmental Review 370, as cited in Judicial Assessment, *supra*, footnote 37, at p. 999.

[40] See David P.H. Jones, "The Evidence of a Three-Year Old Child", [1987] Crim. L.R. 677 at p. 681. See also Westcott, *supra*, footnote 38, at p. 204; Lamb, *supra*, footnote 38, at p. 38.

[41] Judicial Assessment, *supra*, footnote 37, at p. 999.

[42] Underwager and Wakefield, *supra*, footnote 38, at pp. 28-9. For further reading on this issue, see also Olafson, *supra*, footnote 38, at pp. 14-31; Lamb, *supra*, footnote 38, at pp. 50-57; Judicial Assessment, *supra*, footnote 37, at p. 999.

affirmative, as they will rarely respond with "I don't know."[43] An early study provided the following view:

> The most successful strategies for obtaining accurate descriptive recall were found to be encouraging and acceptance of unprompted description, accompanied by sparing use of general questions to prompt recall. Questioning for specific details is likely to result in inaccurate information. Above all, when questioning, it is important to convey as strongly as possible to the child that questions do not have to be answered, moreover, that it is better to say "I don't know" than to give an uncertain answer.[44]

Recent studies have reached similar results, with Nicholas Bala *et al.* noting that in dealing with a child witness, one must overcome the fact that children are socialized to provide answers, even if they are uncertain as to what is being asked of them. The authors suggest the following:

> There are questioning techniques that can increase the accuracy and completeness of the testimony of children, such as showing warmth and support to children, mimicking the vocabulary of the child, avoiding legal jargon, confirming meanings of words with children, limiting use of yes/no questions and avoiding of abstract conceptual questions. As well, preparing children for court and providing them with memory retrieval strategies can increase recall of details.[45]

(c) Aids to Recall and Description

There is some research to support the view that young children recall more completely and more accurately when they are provided with a model of the location where the events occurred and miniatures of some of the objects involved. However, there is also a good deal of concern that demonstrative aids are potentially suggestive and that their use should therefore be avoided.[46] Underwager and Wakefield, for example, have

---

[43] Judicial Assessment, *supra*, footnote 37, at p. 1000.

[44] Helen R. Dent, "The Effects of Interviewing Strategies on the Results of Interviews with Child Witnesses", in A. Trankell, ed., *Reconstructing the Past* (The Netherlands: Kluwer, Deventer, 1982), at p. 292.

[45] Judicial Assessment, *supra*, footnote 37, at p. 1000. See also Karen J. Saywitz and Thomas D. Lyon, "Coming to Grips with Children's Suggestibility" in Mitchell Eisen, Gail S. Goodman and Jodi A. Quas, eds., *Memory and Suggestibility in the Forensic Interview* (Hillsdale, N.J.: Erlbaum, 2001), p. 85.

[46] D.W.W. Price, The Development of Children's Comprehension of Recurring Episodes (unpublished doctoral dissertation, 1983) referred to in Gail S. Goodman, "The Child Witness: Conclusions and Future Directions for

raised serious questions about the possible suggestive effects of some techniques commonly used in the interrogation of children, such as drawings, books, play therapy and anatomically correct dolls.[47]

(d)   Trauma of Testifying

Goodman reports that while many writers put considerable weight on the stress caused to children by the experience of preparing and giving evidence in court, there is little research to support these assertions.[48]

However, there is a good deal of expert evidence reported in the cases supporting the view that testifying in the particular circumstances of those cases will or is likely to be damaging to the child.[49] Moreover, counsel knows that many adults find testifying a difficult experience and it seems unlikely that children would find it less so.

Bala *et al.*'s recent study of judges' perceptions of children's evidence emphasized the need for legal professionals, including defence lawyers who cross examine children and judges who must assess the child's testimony, to be taught how to avoid intimidation and ask questions that are developmentally appropriate and considerate of the fact that the testifying witness is a child, not an adult. Being sensitive to the particular situation of children should not, however, be conflated with a practice of applying a lesser standard of scrutiny to children's evidence. While the rules have been relaxed to enable the easier receipt of children's evidence, counsel should not mistake this development with a practice of what one appellate judge referred to as "an indiscriminate acceptance of the evidence of children".[50] As mentioned earlier, counsel should therefore consider very carefully whether it is essential for the child to testify.

Research and Legal Practice" (1984), 40 Journal of Social Issues 157 at p. 162; for a summary of the concerns and references to some of the relevant literature see Nancy E. Walker and Matthew Nguyen, "Interviewing the Child Witness: The Do's and the Don'ts, the How's and the Why's" (1996), 29 Creighton Law Review 1587.

[47]   Underwager and Wakefield, *supra,* footnote 38, at pp. 30-39.

[48]   Gail S. Goodman, "Children's Testimony in Historical Perspective" (1984) 40 Journal of Social Issues 9, at p. 167; see also *R. v. F. (W.J.),* [1999] 3 S.C.R. 569, 178 D.L.R. (4th) 53, 138 C.C.C. (3d) 1, [1999] 12 W.W.R. 587, 180 Sask. R. 161, 27 C.R. (5th) 169, 247 N.R. 62, 205 W.A.C. 161, 43 W.C.B. (2d) 471, *per* L'Heureux-Dubé J., at para. 14, citing studies which affirm the potentially traumatic effects of testifying.

[49]   Underwager and Wakefield, *supra,* footnote 38, at pp. 30-39. See also Westcott, *supra,* footnote 38, at p. 207; Bill C-2, *supra,* footnote 38, at p. 61.

[50]   Finlayson J.A. in *R. v. S. (W.)* (1994), 90 C.C.C. (3d) 242, 18 O.R. (3d) 509, 70 O.A.C. 370, 29 C.R. (4th) 143, 23 W.C.B. (2d) 372 (Ont. C.A.), leave to

(e) Honesty

Although there are special considerations that counsel should guard against when preparing a child witness, it is important to note that children are generally perceived by the judiciary as honest. Bala *et al.*'s recent study included a survey of judicial perceptions of children's evidence. The overwhelming view was that while children may be subject to suggestibility, or may make mistakes when asked questions that are beyond their cognitive or developmental level, children are generally perceived by judges to be honest witnesses.[51] This suggests that, to the extent that counsel is able to eliminate such factors as confusing questions, leading questions, or questions that are overly complex or repetitive, counsel will be able to get an honest and accurate account from the child.

Remember that the court has a responsibility to ensure that a child witness understands the questions being asked,[52] but it is counsel who must take the lead in helping the court to achieve that objective. This task starts at the preparation stage, by ensuring that the child recognizes the need to answer honestly and only if the child understands the question and can provide an answer. But counsel's role does not end at the courthouse steps; it continues in the courtroom, both by asking questions in a manner that reflects the child's cognitive abilities and by intervening when opposing counsel does not. Given our evolving understanding of children's cognitive abilities, and the need for further education on the part both of judges and of lawyers in this domain, a trial involving a child witness is not the time for counsel to sit back and hope that the witness will get through the evidence-giving process unscathed.

8.4   WHO SHOULD DO THE INTERVIEWING

There is a large body of scientific literature about the conditions which either add to or detract from the reliability of children's evidence. This, coupled with the fact that a poor interviewing technique may do irreparable harm to the accuracy of the child's evidence, suggests that it may be wise to have a specially trained person conduct the interview of a prospective child witness. This is almost an invariable rule where the

---

appeal to S.C.C. refused 93 C.C.C. (3d) vi, 86 O.A.C. 78*n*, 185 N.R. 398*n sub nom. R. v. Stewart*, cited in Nicholas Bala, Karuna Ramakrishnan, Roderick Lindsay and Kang Lee, "Judicial Assessment of the Credibility of Child Witnesses" (2004-2005), 42 Alta. L. Rev. 995, at p. 1006.

[51] Judicial Assessment, *ibid.*, at p. 1012.

[52] *Ibid.*, at p. 1016.

child is a participant in, or a witness to, a major traumatic event and is at least an idea worth considering where the child's evidence relates to the matters which are less traumatic and less central to the key issues in the case.

8.5   IMPLICATIONS FOR WITNESS PREPARATION

An early determination must be made as to whether a child is to be called as a witness. A threshold consideration is whether the evidence will be admitted having regard to the statutory requirements reviewed earlier in this chapter. If the child is to be called, an important part of the preparation will involve instructing the child with respect to the questions that will be asked to satisfy these requirements.[53] Early consideration should also be given to the possibility that the child's evidence is not essential or that it can be given in some other way than traditional oral testimony in court.[54]

Although many of the authorities and statutory provisions relate to criminal or child welfare cases, some recent enactments, such as the sections of the *Evidence Act* in Ontario, referred to earlier, mean that comparable arrangements are possible in a civil case if the groundwork is properly laid.

Important considerations arise from the concern that children's memories fade more quickly than those of adults and that children's accounts are more likely to be influenced by suggestions from adults. These are two factors which suggest some general rules for interviewing and preparing prospective child witnesses:

1. The child should be interviewed as soon as possible after the incident, within a few days if possible.
2. Special care must be taken not to explicitly or implicitly make suggestions to the child or to give the impression that the questioner expects or wants certain kinds of answers.
3. Questions should be very general and, in Dent's words, should "be encouraging . . . of unprompted description" with "sparing use of general questions to prompt recall".[55] Specific questions should be avoided as they are more likely to elicit inaccurate recollection.

---

[53]   See R.N. Lang, "Preparation of Crown Witnesses for Examination in Chief" (1988), 6 Crown C. Rev. 11 at p. 14.

[54]   Some of these possibilities are outlined in Section 8.2.

[55]   *Supra,* footnote 44, at p. 292. See also Helen L. Westcott, "Child Witness Testimony: What Do We Know and Where Are We Going?" in Belinda Brooks-Gordon and Michael Freeman, eds., *Law and Psychology* (New

4. Counsel should recognize that children's recollections about the core elements of events are more accurate than their recollections about peripheral details. To the extent the peripheral details are irrelevant, do not discount the child's evidence simply because of inconsistencies in such details.

5. The interviewer should stress to the child that it is perfectly alright not to answer a question and better to do that than to provide doubtful information. Given children's propensity to answer a question, even when they do not fully understand the question, counsel must emphasize for the child that "I don't understand" or "I don't know" can be an appropriate answer.

6. Counsel should try to obtain particulars of every occasion on which the matter has been discussed with the child. This will help in the assessment of the extent to which the child's recall has been influenced by suggestions from others.

7. Detailed records of all interviews should be kept. Some authors have suggested that all interviews should be videotaped.[56] This approach has several advantages. It provides the most complete record of the interview that may help demonstrate that the child's evidence was not prompted. The videotape will show the child's demeanour and record his or her gestures, both of which are important aspects of the child's responses. The videotape will also be an excellent method of preserving the child's complete memory of the incident, and one that may be able to be used at a future date. This aspect is highly significant given that children's memories tend to fade more rapidly than those of adults and that trials are often a year or more after the events giving rise to the litigation.

8. The location of the interviews should be carefully considered. The more comfortable and familiar the surroundings are for the child, the better. Consideration should also be given to visiting the location where the incidents in question take place, provided that this is not suggestive of matters that are in dispute, and that it would not be painful or traumatic for the child.

9. Early consideration should be given to having all interviews conducted by someone with the relevant training and experience.

York: Oxford University Press, Inc., 2006), at p. 205 and Erna Olafson, "Children's Memory and Suggestibility" in Kathleen Coulborn Faller, ed., *Interviewing Children About Sexual Abuse: Controversies and Best Practices* (New York: Oxford University Press, Inc., 2007), at p. 12.

[56] See, for example, Heino Lilles, "Children As Witnesses: Some Legal and Psychological Viewpoints" (1986), 5 Can. J. Fam. L. 237 at p. 249.

10. If the child is to be called as a witness, counsel should provide instruction on the initial requirements of the oath and understanding of the duty to tell the truth, so that the child is prepared to deal with the court's questions about these matters.

11. A visit to the courtroom is essential so that the child will begin to be less uncomfortable in those surroundings.

12. Consideration should be given to special arrangements with the court and opposing counsel for the child's testimony; these should be settled before the child comes to court. Opposing counsel should be put on notice that you will object if questions are asked that are beyond the child's cognitive or developmental abilities. To the extent necessary, ask the judge to intervene where it is unclear whether the child understands a question.

Walker and Nguyen have provided a list of do's and don'ts which also may be helpful:[57]

Do:

- Prepare for the interview
- Create an appropriate climate for the interview
- Use developmentally appropriate language
- Establish rapport
- Explain the interview purpose
- Discuss the interview ground rules
- Request a free narrative
- Ask direct questions only if necessary
- Explain legal proceedings
- Formally close the interview

Don't:

- Use demonstrative aids
- Use leading questions
- Modify the child's statements
- Use multi-part questions
- Use forced-choice questions

---

[57] Nancy E. Walker and Matthew Nguyen, "Interviewing the Child Witness: The Do's and the Don'ts, the How's and the Why's" (1996), 29 Creighton Law Review 1587, reprinted with permission. Copyright ©1996 by Creighton University.

9

WITNESS PREPARATION
AND PROFESSIONAL
RESPONSIBILITY

9.1 INTRODUCTION

Witness preparation is at the heart of the judicial fact-finding process. Thorough preparation is essential for the proper presentation of the client's case and for the smooth operation of the trial. However, preparation of witnesses gives rise to serious ethical questions mainly concerning tension between the obligations to the client and the dangers of improperly distorting the fact-finding process.

As in many areas of professional conduct, it is difficult to give definitive answers to all the questions. An overview of some of the basic issues is provided in the following sections.[1]

9.2 THE OBLIGATION TO INTERVIEW

The beginning point is that there is no property in a witness. It is perfectly proper for counsel to approach and interview any potential witness. Professional conduct guidelines impose three caveats to this

---

[1] See Gavin MacKenzie, *Lawyers & Ethics: Professional Responsibility and Discipline*, Looseleaf ed. (Toronto: Carswell, 1993), s. 4.12; Alan Mewett, Q.C. and Peter J. Sankoff, *Witnesses*, Looseleaf ed. (Toronto: Carswell, 1991), ch. 6 at s. 6.2; John S. Applegate, "Witness Preparation" (1989), 68 Texas L. Rev. 277; Joseph S. Pioskowski, "Professional Conduct and the Preparation of Witnesses for Trial: Defining the Acceptable Limits of 'Concluding'" (1987), 1 Geo. J. Legal Ethics 389.

general rule. First, the lawyer should disclose his or her true position in the matter. Second, care must be taken to avoid tampering with the evidence or any suggestion that the witness would be unavailable for trial. Third, where a person is represented by counsel, your approach must be through counsel and not to the person directly.[2]

Not only is it important to interview witnesses, but failure to interview may constitute negligence and/or professional misconduct. A lawyer is to offer advice "based on a sufficient knowledge of the relevant facts".[3] Interviewing potential witnesses is probably not necessary in all situations. For example, it may not be necessary in formulating many preliminary opinions. However, witness interviewing may be essential in other situations. In one case, a lawyer was found to be negligent when he provided advice to his clients about settlement of a motor vehicle accident case without interviewing an independent eyewitness where that evidence was helpful to his clients' position.[4] Both a lawyer's ethical responsibilities and the duty of care in representing clients in litigation make interviewing witnesses critical at least in some situations.

9.3 THE ETHICAL LIMITS OF WITNESS PREPARATION

The conventional wisdom is that proper preparation of a witness for testifying may include:

(a) advising the witness which things to emphasize and which to address only if specifically asked;

(b) cautioning a witness not to say more than necessary or urging a witness to be less reticent; and

(c) pointing out to the witness the difference between knowledge and surmise.[5]

---

[2] See, for example, The Law Society of Upper Canada, *Rules of Professional Conduct* (as amended to April 22, 2010), Rule 6.03(7), available online at: http://www.lsuc.on.ca/media/rpc.pdf. See also *R. v. Chapman* (1958), 26 W.W.R. 385 at p. 393 (B.C.C.A.); *Transamerican Life Insurance Co. v. Seward* (1997), 33 O.R. (3d) 604 at p. 609, 71 A.C.W.S. (3d) 773 (Gen. Div.).

[3] Law Society of Upper Canada, *ibid.*, Commentary accompanying Rule 2.02(1); *cf.* MacKenzie, *supra*, footnote 1, at s. 4.12.

[4] *Fawell v. Atkins* (1981), 28 B.C.L.R. 32 (S.C.), as discussed in B.G. Smith, *Professional Conduct for Lawyers and Judges*, 2d ed. (Fredericton: Maritime Law Book, 1998), ch. 6, para. 33.

[5] See Smith, *ibid.*, at ch. 6, para. 32, quoting with approval M.M. Orkin, *Legal*

In general, the conventional wisdom places the line between making the evidence relevant and effective which is permissible, and tampering with the evidence, which is not. As a matter of practice, the distinction is not an easy one to draw or to enforce. In an insightful article, Monroe Freedman shows how artificial the conventional wisdom is.[6] Freedman points out that the process of memory is not a simple matter of resurrecting fixed traces, but instead a process of "creative reconstruction". The reconstruction of past events is highly susceptible to distortion through, for example, bias, self-interest, form of questioning, language of questioning and many other factors. The process of describing the law or saying what is important, both of which are often necessary during preparation, may distort the witness's "recollection" even where the witness is trying to be completely honest. Freedman describes the lawyer's dilemma as follows:

> On the one hand, we know that by telling the client that a particular fact is important, and why it is important, we may induce the client to "remember" the fact even if it did not occur. On the other hand, important facts can truly be lost if we fail to provide the client with every possible aid to memory. Furthermore, since the client's memory is inevitably going to be affected by reconstruction consistent with self-interest, a client who has a misunderstanding of his or her own legal interest could be psychologically inclined to remember in a way that is not only inconsistent with the client's case, but also inaccurate.[7]

Some examples help illustrate these points:

Example 1: X is charged with armed robbery. He tells his counsel that he was the driver of the car, but did not participate in the robbery. Defence counsel is aware of two witnesses who can place X at the scene in the car. Counsel also believes that the police have not spoken to these witnesses. At the trial, the Crown evidence placing X at the scene is ruled inadmissible. After the Crown closes its case, X and his counsel confer. X intends to give evidence and asks counsel if the Crown is aware of the two

---

Ethics: A Study of Professional Conduct (Toronto: Cartwright & Sons, 1957).

[6] Monroe H. Freedman, "Counselling the Client: Refreshing Recollection or Prompting Perjury?", ch. 6, in *Lawyer's Ethics in an Adversary System* (Indianapolis: Bobbs-Merrill, 1975).

[7] *Ibid.*, at pp. 68-9. Reprinted with permission of the Macmillan Publishing Company.

witnesses that could place him at the scene.[8]

This example raises several ethical issues, one of which is whether counsel should answer the client's question. The client's question seems calculated to discover whether there is evidence to contradict the client's potential false testimony that he was not at the scene. The lawyer answering the question might be seen as assisting the client to commit perjury. However, it seems to us that counsel investigated the matter on behalf of the client and the client is entitled to know the results of counsel's efforts. Completely different considerations arise if the witness announces an intention to give evidence that counsel knows is false or perjures himself while testifying.

> **Example 2:** The client is charged with murder. At the outset of the interview, counsel makes some general comments about the charge and the procedure to be followed and then says: "The law is that if you were drunk or acted out of blind rage, the charge should be reduced to manslaughter."[9]

This example raises the problem of where advice about the law ends and encouraging perjury begins. No one doubts that it is the lawyer's duty to give a client advice about the law. But it is also a lawyer's duty not to "knowingly assist in or encourage any dishonesty, fraud, crime or illegal conduct, or instruct the client on how to violate the law and avoid punishment".[10] The issue turns, then, on the purpose for which the advice is being given.

In the example, the information is offered by the lawyer before the client inquires and without eliciting even a bare outline of the facts from the client. In these circumstances, it is hard to know what purpose the advice could have other than to assist the client to manufacture evidence. Freedman's comments on this issue are helpful:

> In interviewing, therefore, the attorney must take into account the practical psychological realities of the situation. That means, at least at the earlier stages of eliciting the client's story, that the attorney should assume a skeptical attitude, and that the attorney should give the client legal advice that might help in drawing out useful information that the client, consciously or unconsciously, might be withholding. To that extent — but on a different, and more limiting, rationale — I adhere to my earlier position that there are situations in which it may be proper for the attorney

---

[8] Based on an example given in A. Kenneth Pye, "The Role of Counsel in the Suppression of Truth" (1978), Duke Law Journal 921 at p. 928.

[9] See Freedman, *supra*, footnote 6, at p. 69.

[10] Law Society of Upper Canada, *supra*, footnote 2, Rule 2.02(5).

to give the client legal advice even though the attorney has reason to believe that the advice may induce the client to commit perjury. There does come a point, however, where nothing less than "brute rationalization" can purport to justify a conclusion that the lawyer is seeking in good faith to elicit truth rather than actively participating in the creation of perjury.[11]

Example 3: Interview of potential witness in a motor vehicle case.
Lawyer: I've been told the green Toyota was flying. How fast was it going when it smashed into the truck?
Witness: At least 80 km/h.
Lawyer: Could it have been more?
Witness: Yes, it was flying alright.

We discussed in an earlier section the potential impact of the form of the questions and the choice of language on the response obtained from the witness. In this example, the use of the words "flying" and "smash", along with the leading form of the questions could easily contribute to the nature of the witness's response and might distort the witness's reconstruction of the events. Whether this constitutes professional misconduct under the various codes is unclear, but it seems that it is improper and unwise to use highly suggestive forms of questioning and choice of language. These techniques may not only leave counsel with a very misleading picture, but may also unduly influence the witness's attempt to reconstruct the events.

9.4   PRESENTING WITNESSES

The general ethical guidelines concerning witnesses are well known. Counsel must not knowingly suppress evidence or adduce false or misleading evidence. The Rules of Professional Conduct of The Law Society of Upper Canada deal with these subjects as follows:

The lawyer must not . . .

  (e)   knowingly attempt to deceive a tribunal or influence the course of justice by offering false evidence . . . suppressing what ought to be disclosed . . .

      . . . . .

  (i)   dissuade a witness from giving evidence or advise a witness to be absent;

---

[11] Freedman, *supra*, footnote 6, at p. 75. Reprinted with permission of the Macmillan Publishing Company.

(j)   knowingly permit a witness or party to be presented in a false or misleading way or to impersonate another.[12]

The problem of the witness who, to counsel's knowledge, may or in fact does commit perjury has been thoroughly discussed in many places. Nothing would be served by adding to those discussions here other than to make the point that the witness who does commit perjury gives rise to one of the toughest ethical dilemmas and one to which a variety of proper solutions have been advanced. There are some other less thoroughly canvassed and more common ethical problems:

1.   What is the extent of counsel's duty to adduce unfavourable evidence?
2.   What is the extent of counsel's duty not to unduly inconvenience a witness?
3.   What rules govern communication between counsel and the witness once the testimony has begun?

(a)   The Duty to Adduce Evidence

Counsel will exert strict control over what evidence is adduced on the client's behalf. This will include selecting witnesses and establishing the topics on which they will testify. Of course, there are clear limits on the ability of counsel to select or limit evidence. This is particularly true in civil matters in which there are clear obligations to produce all relevant documentation, and of course, a witness, once called, may be cross-examined on all relevant matters, including issues of credibility.

With these clear situations aside, is counsel obliged to disclose or adduce unfavourable evidence? The answer is yes in at least two situations: where the proceeding is *ex parte*, and where failure to lead the evidence would mislead the tribunal.

In general, it is not part of counsel's role in adversary proceedings to assist the opponent to prove his or her case. This is recognized in the various codes of professional conduct which usually stipulate that, except where provided by law, it is not the advocate's role "to assist an adversary or advance matters derogatory to the client's case".[13] One important exception to this general rule consists of situations in which, to use the words of the Ontario rule, "the full proof and argument inherent in the

---

[12]   The Law Society of Upper Canada, *supra*, footnote 2, Rule 4.01(2).
[13]   *Ibid.*, commentary accompanying Rule 4.01(1).

adversary system cannot be achieved".[14] These situations include *ex parte* and uncontested matters. In these cases, counsel must be completely candid and present the relevant evidence both favourable and unfavourable. To use the words of the code, "the lawyer must take particular care to be accurate, candid and comprehensive in presenting the client's case so as to ensure that the tribunal is not misled".[15] We think that this obligation requires counsel to take all reasonable steps during the preparation as well as governing the manner of presentation of the evidence. It is not enough to elicit only favourable information during preparation so that ignorance prevents disclosure of damaging information. Ignorance is not bliss when it could have been reasonably avoided and where the ignorance results in the court being deprived of relevant material.

A more controversial question is that of counsel's duty to adduce unfavourable evidence in a fully adversarial proceeding. Our view is that there is no ethical obligation to adduce such evidence short of a case where failure to do so makes the evidence given false or misleading. Although the line is not easy to draw, we think there is a difference between presenting the court with accurate information on one subject and none on another, and presenting the court with one-half of the accurate information on one subject. The former is permitted under the adversary system; the latter is not.

Some authorities would impose a higher obligation. Professor Beverley Smith, in his text *Professional Conduct for Lawyers and Judges*,[16] addresses the issue of whether counsel is under a duty to bring forward a witness who can only harm the client's case. He concludes that given "the pre-eminent duty of the lawyer to serve the cause of justice, the correct course would be to make the witness available to the court while acknowledging that his evidence likely cannot assist in establishing the case of the lawyer's client".[17] This view has some textual support in the Rules of Professional Conduct which speak of a lawyer's duty not to suppress "what ought to be disclosed".[18] Professor Smith also relies by analogy on counsel's obligation to advise the court of pertinent adverse

---

[14] *Ibid.*

[15] *Ibid.*

[16] B.G. Smith, *Professional Conduct for Lawyers and Judges*, 2nd ed. (Fredericton: Maritime Law Book, 1998).

[17] *Ibid.*, at ch. 7, para. 47ff.

[18] The Law Society of Upper Canada, *Rules of Professional Conduct* (as amended to April 22, 2010), Rule 4.01(2)(e), available online at: http://www.lsuc.on.ca/media/rpc.pdf.

case law.[19] With respect, we think this places the duty too high and distorts the adversary process.

As the Rules point out, the advocate's role is necessarily partisan and there is no duty to assist an adversary or to advance matters derogatory to the client's case. Provided all obligations to provide discovery have been scrupulously adhered to, counsel need not make adverse witnesses available or lead damaging evidence, unless the omission constitutes dishonesty. We think that if a witness is called, the examination-in-chief should deal fairly with all the subjects touched upon, but counsel calling the witness is under no obligation to bring out unhelpful evidence not part of the client's case or to make unfavourable witnesses who are not called available to the court.

(b)   The Duty Not to Inconvenience a Witness

The Rules of Professional Conduct state, without elaboration, that the lawyer must not "needlessly inconvenience a witness".[20] This obligation should be uppermost in counsel's mind throughout the preparation and the trial itself. To reiterate, a number of points about how witnesses should be treated are:

(a)   counsel must be honest with the witness about his or her client's position;

(b)   estimates of time involved for preparation must be realistic;

(c)   appointments must be as convenient as possible and must be kept; and

(d)   every reasonable effort must be taken to give the witness adequate notice of when the evidence will be heard and all reasonable efforts must be taken to avoid unnecessary waiting around the courtroom.

These are no more than basic courtesy and, given the importance of witnesses to the client, considerate treatment of witnesses is also good strategy.

(c)   Communication With Witnesses During and After Testimony

Custom and rules of professional conduct govern communication with witnesses during and after testimony. The details of these rules vary

---

[19]   *Ibid.*, Rule 4.01(2)(h).
[20]   *Ibid.*, Rule 4.01(2)(m).

somewhat from jurisdiction to jurisdiction. Rule 4.04 of the Ontario Rules of Professional Conduct establishes the following:

> 4.04 Subject to the direction of the tribunal, the lawyer shall observe the following rules respecting communication with witnesses giving evidence:
>
> (a) during examination-in-chief, the examining lawyer may discuss with the witness any matter that has not been covered in the examination up to that point,
>
> (b) during examination-in-chief by another legal practitioner of a witness who is unsympathetic to the lawyer's cause, the lawyer not conducting the examination-in-chief may discuss the evidence with the witness,
>
> (c) between completion of examination-in-chief and commencement of cross-examination of the lawyer's own witness, the lawyer ought not to discuss the evidence given in chief or relating to any matter introduced or touched on during the examination-in-chief,
>
> (d) during cross-examination by an opposing legal practitioner, the witness's own lawyer ought not to have any conversation with the witness about the witness's evidence or any issue in the proceeding,
>
> (e) between completion of cross-examination and commencement of re-examination, the lawyer who is going to re-examine the witness ought not to have any discussion about evidence that will be dealt with on re-examination,
>
> (f) during cross-examination by the lawyer of a witness unsympathetic to the cross-examiner's cause, the lawyer may discuss the witness's evidence with the witness,
>
> (g) during cross-examination by the lawyer of a witness who is sympathetic to that lawyer's cause, any conversations ought to be restricted in the same way as communications during examination-in-chief of one's own witness, and
>
> (h) during re-examination of a witness called by an opposing legal practitioner, if the witness is sympathetic to the lawyer's cause the lawyer ought not to discuss the evidence to be given by that witness during re-examination. The lawyer may, however, properly discuss the evidence with a witness who is adverse in interest.[21]

The Commentary that accompanies the above states that if there is any question whether the lawyer's behaviour may be in violation of this rule of conduct, it will often be appropriate to obtain the consent of the opposing lawyer and leave of the court before engaging in conversations that may be considered improper or a breach of etiquette.[22] When there has been an order excluding witnesses, it is improper for counsel to relate to an

[21] *Ibid.*, Rule 4.04.

[22] See also Mewett and Sankoff, *supra*, footnote 1, at s. 6.3; Brian McLaughlin, "When May Counsel Talk to an Adverse Witness During Trial" (1989), 47

excluded witness any of the testimony of another witness. We think it is not improper to review areas about which the excluded witness may testify and which were covered by other witnesses so long as counsel does not explicitly or by implication relate the testimony of other witnesses. The exclusion order may create practical problems, especially for expert witnesses who may need to be aware of the other evidence in the case. These problems should be considered in advance so that appropriate exceptions to the exclusion order may be made.[23] If a problem arises unexpectedly, the correct approach is, as the Commentary suggests, to seek consent from opposing counsel and leave of the court for your communication with the witness.

The Advocate 237; John Sopinka, D.B. Houston and M. Sopinka, *The Trial of an Action* (Markham: Butterworths, 1998), at p. 126ff.

[23] The court will usually allow counsel to have one expert present while an expert is giving evidence on the other side.

Appendix A

MEMORANDUM FOR WITNESSES — TESTIFYING IN COURT

This memorandum is designed to provide you with some basic information about being a witness in court. Witnesses are important to the party calling them to testify and to the justice system. The main obligation of a witness is to tell the truth to the best of his or her ability. Everything else said in this memorandum is secondary to that overriding obligation.

1. PREPARATION

Your testimony is important and you will need to be fully prepared in order to make your evidence as complete and easy to understand and effective as possible. You will need to commit the time necessary to complete this preparation. Every effort will be made not to inconvenience you unduly, but you will have to arrange your schedule to permit time for adequate preparation.

2. BEFORE BEING CALLED TO THE STAND

Our systems of scheduling trials make it difficult to know exactly when the case will begin. Once the case begins, the pace at which it will proceed is impossible to predict with certainty.

We will make every effort to give you the best estimate possible of when your evidence will be heard. But please remember there are many variables which are not under our control and all we can do is keep in close contact as the trial approaches.

It is very common for a trial judge to make an order excluding all witnesses other than the one testifying from the courtroom. This order also requires that witnesses not discuss their evidence with each other during the trial. Failure to obey this order could be contempt of court and may have serious consequences for the case. Please do not discuss the case with anyone but counsel once the trial begins.

3. THE OATH

When your evidence is required, the clerk or bailiff will call your name, you will come into court and proceed to the witness stand. You may remain standing for your testimony, but usually witnesses are seated while giving evidence. The clerk of the court will then administer the oath on the Bible or other religious text in which you promise to tell the truth. You may also solemnly affirm to tell the truth if you do not wish to take an oath. Regardless of which process you take, what you must recall is this: you must answer all questions honestly. *It is a serious criminal offence knowingly to give false evidence.*

4. ORDER AND SCOPE OF QUESTIONING

Once you are sworn, the lawyer for the party calling you will ask questions. This is called "Examination-in-Chief" or "Direct Examination". Generally speaking, the questions during this part of the evidence will be rather open-ended and not leading.

It is very important that you listen to the question and wait until the whole question has been put before you begin your answer.

When the examination-in-chief is over, counsel for all opposing parties may cross-examine. Cross-examination may deal with areas not covered in chief and counsel may ask questions which suggest an answer and ask you to agree or disagree.

You should answer the questions to the best of your ability, telling the whole truth. We have a few rules of thumb for helping you with cross-examination which we will set out later in this memo.

Once the cross-examination has begun, you must not discuss your evidence with anyone, including the lawyer who called you as a witness.

After all parties who are entitled to do so have had an opportunity to cross-examine, the lawyer who called you as a witness may ask some further questions. This is known as re-examination. Questioning is limited to clarifying matters raised during the cross-examination and, once again, counsel may not ask leading questions.

At any point during the witness's testimony, the presiding judge may ask questions. You should answer these questions in a straightforward and truthful way, but you should not let the judge put words in your mouth unless they accurately express your own best recollection.

You should answer every question that is asked if you can. You should say you do not know the answer or that you do not understand the question if that is the case. It is your job to answer the questions, not to judge or comment on the propriety or relevance of the questions. Counsel who called you as a witness will object to any improper questions and opposing counsel may also make objections. Once an objection has been made to a question, you should keep silent until directed to answer by the judge or until a new question has been put forward.

5. SOME HELPFUL HINTS FOR CROSS-EXAMINATION

(a) Listen carefully to the question. Make sure you understand the question. If you do not understand the question, say so.

(b) Answer the question asked and none other. Give a complete answer but do not volunteer any information not required by the question.

(c) Do not guess at an answer. If you do not know the answer, say so.

(d) Do not concern yourself at all with where the question is leading. Concentrate only on the question asked and the giving of an accurate and complete answer.

(e) Be polite, even in the face of aggressive questioning.

(f) Tell the truth to the best of your recollection.

(g) You may be asked whether you discussed your evidence with anyone. Tell the truth. There is nothing improper about discussing your evidence with counsel beforehand.

(h) Do not look to the lawyer who has called you as if for help.

(i) Do not let words be put in your mouth. Use your own words.

6. CONCLUSION

There are many other points that your counsel will deal with before you testify. This memorandum is intended only as an introduction to some of the basic points you should know. Do not hesitate to discuss any questions about the process with counsel.

Appendix B

EXAMINATION FOR DISCOVERY

This memorandum, in the form of questions and answers, has been prepared to help clients understand and prepare for a very important step in their litigation, the examination for discovery.

Q. What is an examination for discovery?

A. An examination for discovery is a pre-trial procedure which allows each party to the litigation to ask questions of any adverse party. The party being examined is under oath.

Q. What is the purpose of an examination for discovery?

A. An examination for discovery serves a number of purposes. The examination allows each side to find out about the other side's case. The party being examined may make admissions which weaken his or her case or which strengthen the case of the other side. These admissions may be used at trial.

Q. Who is in attendance?

A. The person being examined attends with his or her lawyer. The lawyers for the other parties will attend. Usually, the parties will not be in attendance during each other's examination. A stenographer or audio or video technician will be in attendance to record the questions and answers. A judge is not in attendance.

Q. What takes place during the examination?

A. The party being examined will take an oath or affirmation to tell the truth. The lawyer for the adverse party will then ask questions. Not all questions are proper; for example, a question which is totally irrelevant to the subject-matter of the litigation is not proper. If there are grounds to do so, the lawyer for the party being examined may object to the question. Unless his or her lawyer objects, the party being examined should answer the questions. The questions may take the form of cross-examination. The most usual form of cross-examination is a question which suggests a particular answer.

Q. At an examination for discovery do you have to disclose the names of your witnesses?

A. If asked, you have to disclose the names and addresses of persons who might reasonably be expected to have knowledge of transactions or occurrences in issue in the action. If such persons are your witnesses, you have to disclose their names and addresses.

Q. Where does the examination take place?

A. There are officials throughout Ontario known as Official Examiners. The examination may take place at the office of an Official Examiner. Where the parties agree, the examination may take place elsewhere, for example in a lawyer's office.

Q. How long will it take?

A. It varies from case to case. Sometimes an examination takes as little as 20 minutes. Some examinations have taken weeks. New amendments to the Ontario Rules of Civil Procedure have shortened the time for examination to seven hours per party unless the court permits a longer time.

Q. How important is preparation for the examination for discovery?

A. Preparation is very important. While the great majority of actions are settled before trial, most actions proceed through an examination for discovery. Thus in a real sense a good performance on an examination for discovery may be the most important service that a client can do for his or her own case. A bad performance may effectively mean the end of the client's claim or defence.

Q. How should a client prepare for an examination for discovery?

A. The client should review all of his or her documents relevant to the case. The client should inform him or herself of any information relevant to the case which may be available from associates, partners, employees, agents, etc. Prior to the examination, the client will meet with his or her lawyer to review the events giving rise to the litigation and the associated documents. At this meeting the lawyer and client will discuss the nature of the questions which may be anticipated. The lawyer and client will also discuss questions which should be asked of the other side.

Q. Are there any do's and don'ts at the examinations?

A. Yes –

1. Do tell the truth.

2. Do listen very carefully to the question being asked.

3. If you do not understand the question, say so.

4. Answer the question you are asked completely. Do not volunteer information.

5. Do not ramble, be complete but be precise and to the point.

6. Do not guess. If you do not know an answer say so.

7. Do keep calm and composed. You are not alone.

8. Do not argue, joke or plead with the other lawyer.

9. Do not rush. It is not a race.

10. If your lawyer objects to a question, follow his or her direction without an argument or debate.

Q. What happens after the examination?

A. Usually after all the parties have been examined for discovery but sometimes after each examination, the lawyers for the parties will discuss the prospects of settlement. These discussions are usually informal and often take place without the clients being in attendance.

Q. What follow-up is there to the examination for discovery?

A. If the litigation does not settle, typed transcripts of the examinations for discovery will be ordered. Under the Rules of Civil Procedure, you must review your transcript in order to determine whether any of the answers are incorrect or incomplete or whether the answers have become incorrect or incomplete because you have discovered additional information. Often undertakings or promises to obtain further information are given during an examination and these undertakings must be honoured.

121

INDEX